Contemporary Social Studies Series

INDUSTRIAL SOCIETY

Kenneth Duncan, Bruce Urquhart

Oliver & Boyd

Acknowledgements

The publishers wish to thank the following for permission to reproduce photographs or other coypright material on the pages listed:

Bill Clark (p. 1); Vauxhall Motors Ltd (p. 5); London Features International Ltd (A, p. 6); Popperfoto (B, p. 6); Format/ Maggie Murray (C, p. 6); Methodist Church Division of Ministries (D, p. 6); BBC Copyright (p. 8); Royal Commission on Ancient Monuments, Scotland (A, p. 14; B, p. 26); British Steel Corporation (p. 13); Format/Jenny Matthews (B, p. 18); Trustees of the National Library of Scotland (A, p. 22: from H Stephens, *Book of the Farm*, 1851); National Museum of Antiquities of Scotland (B, p. 22); Massey Ferguson (C, p. 22); Baxter Nisbet/Auchindrain Folklife Museum, Inverary (p. 24; D, p. 25); Crown copyright reproduced by permission of the Scottish Development Department (C, p. 25); Kenneth Duncan (C, D, p. 27; B, C, D, p. 29); reproduced by courtesy of the Trustees of the British Museum (A, p. 29); George Outram (p. 31); News Group Newspapers Ltd (A, p. 34, E, p. 35); Mirror Group Newspapers Ltd (B, p. 34); Press Association (C, p. 35); Central Press Photos Ltd (D, p. 35); Mullard Ltd (A, p. 40); Nottingham Building Society (p. 41); Rediffusion (B, p. 42); *New Society* (C, p. 42); Mansell Collection (I, J, p. 43); Strathleven Bond (K, p. 43); Milk Marketing Board (L, p. 43); Austin Rover Group Ltd (pp. 44–5); Times Newspapers Ltd (cartoon, p. 46); Format/Raissa Page (C, p. 46).

Cover photographs by Michael Wolchover, Edinburgh.

Illustration B on p. 5 is based on an illustration which appeared in *The Sunday Times*, 6 November 1983, with the permission of Times Newspapers Ltd.
Sketch A on p. 24 is based on an illustration by Colin Hendry in *A Farming Township: Auchindrain, Argyll*, Alexander Fenton (Perth 1979).
Sketch F on p. 27 is based on an illustration in *New Lanark: Heritage Trail*, New Lanark Conservation and Civic Trust.
Map A on p. 26 is based on the first edition Ordnance Survey 25 inch map, 1863.
Map E on p. 27 is based on Ordnance Survey 1:50 000 sheet 71 with the permission of the Controller of Her Majesty's Stationery Office. Crown copyright reserved.
Extracts C on p. 31 are from *Equal at Work?*, Anna Coote (Collins 1979).
Extract D on p. 31 is adapted from an article in the *Glasgow Herald*.

The authors would like to acknowledge the following individuals and sources which were of help to them in producing material for the text: Taylor Nelson Monitor Ltd; *Employment Gazette*; *ILO Economist*; *Social Trends 1984* (HMSO); Strathclyde Regional publications; Mr Chambers, Faslane Naval Base, Dunbartonshire; Mr Arnold, New Lanark Conservation and Civic Trust; Bob Smith, Auchindrain Folklife Museum, Inveraray; Nottingham Building Society; Austin Rover Group Ltd; Hermione Spencer; Equal Opportunities Commission; Miss H. Monk, Debenhams PLC; the late Robert Young, Keir Estate Dunblane.

Illustrated by Tim Smith, Tony Herbert, John Lobban and Michael Strand

Oliver & Boyd
Robert Stevenson House
1–3 Baxter's Place
Leith Walk
Edinburgh EH1 3BB

A division of Longman Group UK Ltd

ISBN 0 05 003936 9
First published 1986
Second (revised) impression 1988

Set in 12/14pt Helvetica Roman & Light

Produced by Longman Group (F.E.) Ltd
Printed in Hong Kong

Contents

We need each other

Most people in Britain are **producers**. They may work in factories making goods such as cars or televisions. They may provide a **service** for others, by cleaning, teaching or nursing, for example. We all use the services and buy the goods produced by other people: we are **consumers**. Everyone has a part to play in **society** and we all depend on others. Diagram A shows some of the ways money makes people **dependent** on others.

Sajid works in a car assembly plant. Nasreen, his wife, does the housework and looks after their children.

Jean works as a nurse. Ted, her husband, is unemployed. He does the housework and looks after the children.

A

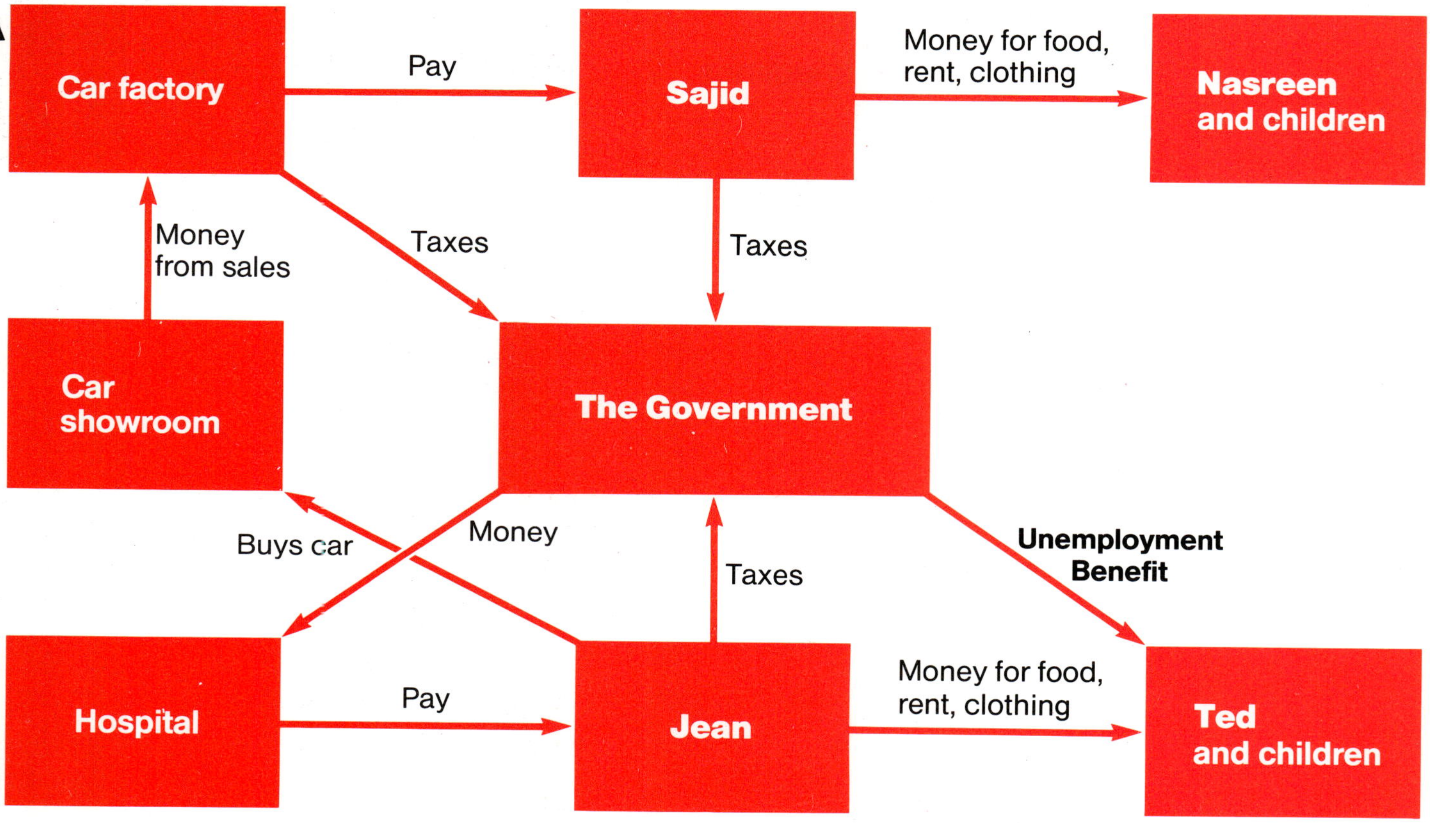

Car factory → **Pay** → Sajid → **Money for food, rent, clothing** → **Nasreen and children**

Car showroom → **Money from sales** → Car factory

Car factory → **Taxes** → The Government

Sajid → **Taxes** → The Government

Money → Car showroom

Car showroom → **Buys car** → Hospital

The Government → **Money** → Hospital

Hospital → **Pay** → Jean

Jean → **Taxes** → The Government

Jean → **Money for food, rent, clothing** → **Ted and children**

The Government → **Unemployment Benefit** → **Ted and children**

Sajid works in the Vauxhall car plant at Luton. This is what he says about his job.

'To make a motor car, a large number of parts are brought together and assembled. The car is put together piece by piece on the assembly line. Different teams of workers fit different parts of the car as it travels along in front of them. As diagram B shows, we depend on other British **firms** and foreign firms to supply us with parts. Without them there could be no car.

I work near the end of the assembly line, fixing the car seats in position. I can now do this one task quickly and accurately.

If any of my mates at an earlier stage on the line fails to do their job then it holds up mine. We all depend on each other.'

Many different types of goods are made on assembly lines. They are said to be **mass produced**. They can be made quickly and efficiently in very large numbers. This means they are cheaper to buy than goods which are made one by one. But companies which made mass-produced goods depend on non-stop production. A breakdown of machinery or a stop in work can cost the company thousands of pounds each day.

B Made in Britain – or is it?

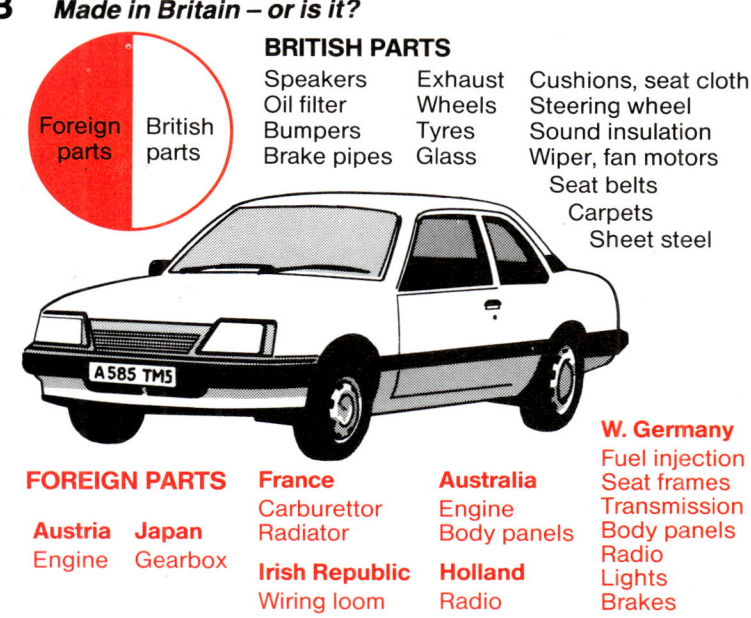

BRITISH PARTS

Speakers	Exhaust	Cushions, seat cloth
Oil filter	Wheels	Steering wheel
Bumpers	Tyres	Sound insulation
Brake pipes	Glass	Wiper, fan motors
		Seat belts
		Carpets
		Sheet steel

FOREIGN PARTS

Austria
Engine

Japan
Gearbox

France
Carburettor
Radiator

Irish Republic
Wiring loom

Australia
Engine
Body panels

Holland
Radio

W. Germany
Fuel injection
Seat frames
Transmission
Body panels
Radio
Lights
Brakes

C Final assembly of the Vauxhall Cavalier

Work unit

1   Look at diagram A.
(a) What does Jean buy that makes her a consumer?
(b) In what way is Sajid a producer?
(c) What does Nasreen depend on to feed and clothe her family?
(d) In what way does Ted depend on the government?
(e) Why does the government depend on people like Sajid and Jean and the car company?
(f) How does Jean depend on the government for her pay?
(g) Why could it be said that Sajid depends on people like Jean for his pay?

2   (a) In what ways do you think Sajid depends on Nasreen?
(b) Why might Sajid say that he pays Nasreen wages?

3   (a) Look at Diagram B. What percentage of the Vauxhall Cavalier is made in Britain?
(b) Why do workers depend on each other in an assembly line?
(c) How could production on the Cavalier be brought to a standstill (see diagram B)?

4   Why are stops in work very costly to companies who make mass-produced goods?

Why work?

Some people think that a job is only proper 'work' if it is physically tiring, or if something is produced at the end of it. Others think that a job is only proper 'work' if workers are paid a wage to do it, and work regular hours each week. Others think that proper 'work' cannot be fun to do!

Pictures A–D show people doing very different jobs. Do you think these are 'work'?

A

B

C

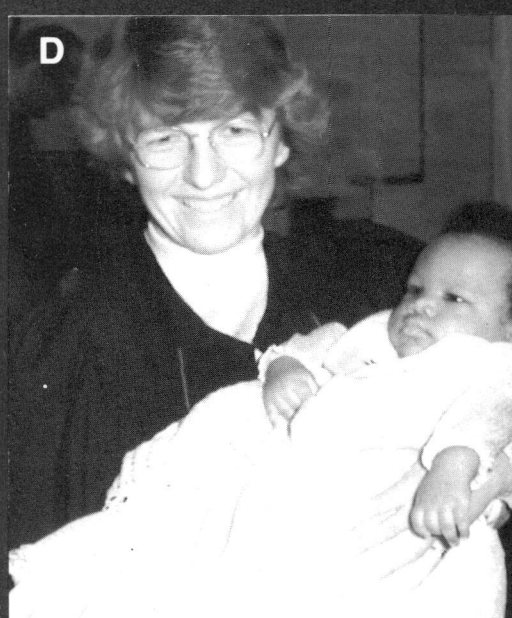

D

Jobs done in the house are often overlooked and not thought to be proper 'work'. This view is usually held by people who do very little around the house! The real value and importance of household work can be seen by working out how much it would cost to pay someone to do this work. At one time, most married women did housework as a full-time unpaid job. Now over 60% of married women have a job outside the home. Because of this, most families have to do housework in their 'free' time or employ others to do the work for them. This has made many people more aware of how much work has to be done in the home.

E

Household work bill

Number of hours

Cooking
Washing up
Shopping
Washing & ironing
Cleaning & tidying
Odd jobs (gardening, etc.)
Child minding
_____
TOTAL HOURS _____

TOTAL COST = total hours × £1.50 = £ _____

In a recent survey carried out in Britain, people were given the six reasons for working shown in diagram F, and asked to put them in order of importance. The most popular ordering is shown below. The 'winning' reason was the leader by a long way.

RESULT

1 You need to work to earn money.
2 Working is interesting and satisfying.
3 You meet people when you work.
4 Working gives you a place in society.
5 Working is something to do.
6 You help society by working.

The survey also looked at how workers in other countries felt about reasons for working. It put workers into three groups according to their views.

1 **Weak view of work:** work only for money (pay).
2 **Strong view of work:** work done is more important than pay.
3 **In-between view of work:** work done and pay are of equal importance.

The results are shown in bar graph G.

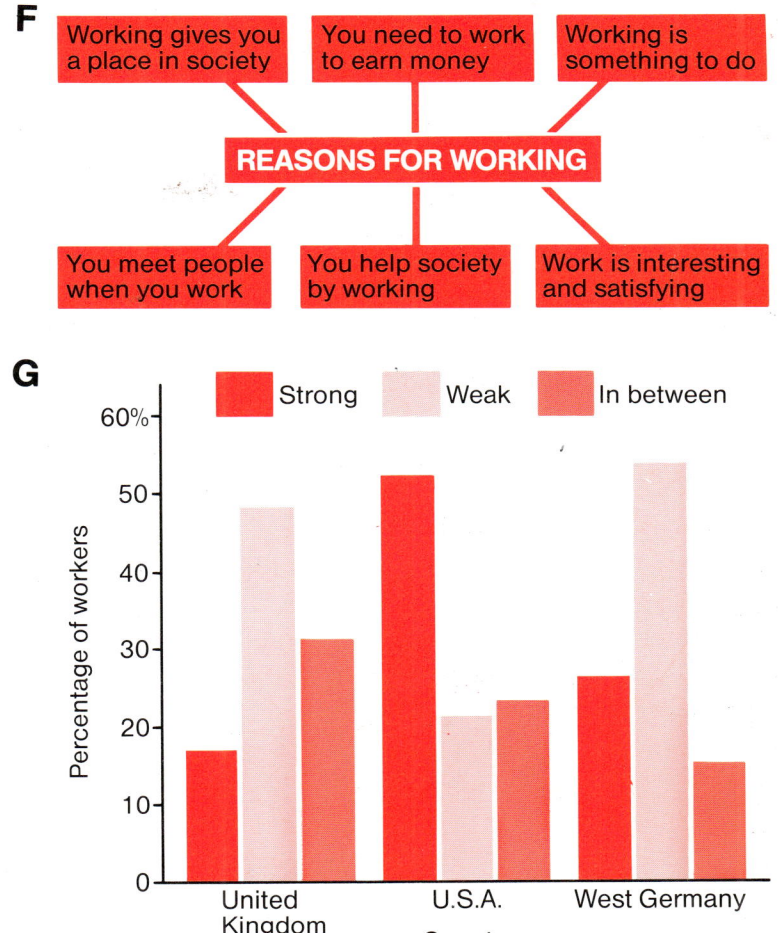

Work unit

1 Look at photographs A–D. For *each* photograph, say
   (a) why the job might not be thought to be 'proper' work,
   (b) why the job can be very hard work.
2 Why are jobs done in the home often not thought of as 'proper' work?
3 Look at the Household work bill (illustration E). Copy it into your notebook. Write in the number of hours spent on each of the jobs listed, in an average week in your home. If a rate of £1.50 per hour was paid for all work done, work out how much your parents would have to spend each week for the household work.
4 What do most British people think is the most important reason for working?
5 Look at graph G.
   (a) In which country do most workers say they work only for the money?

(b) In which country do most workers say that work done is more important than pay?
6 Make up a questionnaire asking people to put the six reasons for working (shown in diagram F) in order of importance. Give copies of your questionnaire to 20 working adults, for them to fill in.

   For each completed questionnaire, award points as follows: 6 points for the first (most important) reason, 5 points for the second most important reason, and so on, giving one point for the least important reason.

   Look at each of the six reasons in turn on all the questionnaires. Add up the total number of points awarded to each reason. Then write out the list of reasons in order of popularity, from the one with the largest total of points to the one with the smallest.

   Do your results agree with the survey?

What is industry?

A

The word **industry** simply means the work that people do. The headlines in **A** show that there are many different industries. The people who work in them form part of **industrial society**.

Firms which make the same kind of goods, or offer the same kind of **service**, are grouped together. For example, train drivers, taxi drivers and bus drivers all work in the transport industry.

There are many different types of job in each industry. Some work needs a special **skill** which must be learned. *Skilled workers* have had months or years of training to do their jobs. *Unskilled work* can be done without training.

Workers who make or fit things with their hands are called *manual workers*. Other workers are called *white-collar workers*. They may work in offices or shops, for example.

Some kinds of work can be found in many different industries. For example, welders are needed in the shipbuilding industry and the car industry. Nearly all industries need office staff.

In recent years unemployment has increased a great deal. Many workers have been made **redundant**. This means they have lost their jobs through no fault of their own. People who are able to work but can't find a job are still part of the **working population**. This means they are as much a part of industrial society as those with jobs.

Work unit

1   Which of the following are industries: fishing, farming, printing, tourism, banking?
2   Which two of the following groups of workers are part of the same industry?
    (a) skilled workers who help make Ford cars
    (b) skilled workers who help make BBC microcomputers
    (c) unskilled workers who help make Dulux paint
    (d) unskilled workers who help make Rolls Royce cars.
    Give reasons for your choice.
3   Read the statements below about industrial society. Write out the ones you think are true.
    (a) Working people do not play a part in industrial society.
    (b) Unemployed people are part of industrial society.
    (c) Only skilled workers are part of industrial society.
    (d) Manual workers are part of industrial society but white-collar workers are not.
    Give reasons for your choice.

B   *Office staff*

Industries can be put into three main groups: *primary* industries, *secondary* industries and *tertiary* industries.

Primary industries

These industries produce materials that are found or grow *naturally*. They provide **raw materials** such as grain, wood, coal and metal which are used by secondary industries.
Examples: farming, fishing, forestry, mining.

Secondary (or manufacturing) industries

These industries use raw materials and **manufacture** or make them into other **products**. The new products may be sold in shops or used by other secondary industries.
Examples: shipbuilding, power supply, bakery, clothing, building.

Tertiary (or service) industries

These industries do not make anything. They provide *services* for people, rather than a *raw material* or a *manufactured product*.
Examples: banking, local and central government, hairdressing, shops, tourism, transport.

Most products go through one or more of the three groups of industry, as picture D shows.

C

FURNITURE

D

Primary

Secondary

Tertiary

Forestry

Furniture manufacture

Furniture shop

Work unit

1 Look again at the newspaper headlines (A) on page 8. Make a table like the one below. Write the industry mentioned in each newspaper headline under the correct heading in the table. One has been done for you.

Primary	Secondary	Tertiary
	Iron and steel industry	

2 Pictures E, F and G show an industry from each of the three main groups (primary, secondary, tertiary).
(a) What is the link between the three industries?
(b) In which order do you think the three industries E, F, G would happen? Explain your choice.
(c) Write down the three picture letters E, F, G in a list. Beside each one write whether it is a primary, secondary or tertiary industry.
(d) Your answers for F and G in question 2(c) should be different. Explain why.

E

F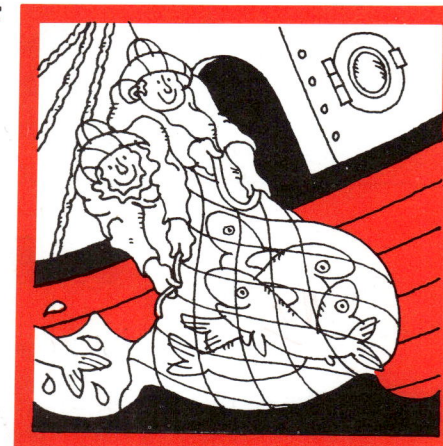

G

As a country *develops* (improves) and becomes wealthier, its industrial needs change. The manufacturing and primary industries usually decrease, while the service industries increase (see diagram H). In less developed countries the highest proportion of workers is usually in primary industry (see Table 1).

The proportions of workers in the three groups of industries vary from one country to another. They also vary from one part of Britain to another, as map I shows.

Table 1 Changes in industry in less developed countries (such as India, China)

Industries	Percentage of workers	
	1960	1980
Primary	73	59
Secondary	13	20
Tertiary	14	21
	100%	100%

H *Employment in different groups of industries in Britain, 1841–1986*

1841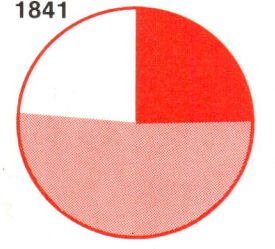
Total: 7 million

1871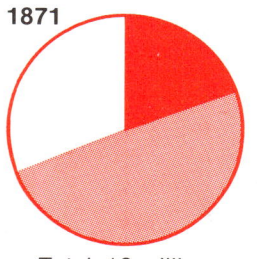
Total: 12 million

1911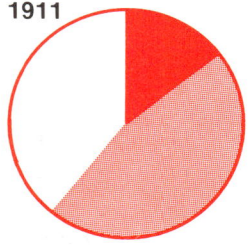
Total: 20 million

1951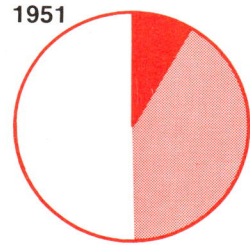
Total: 24 million

1986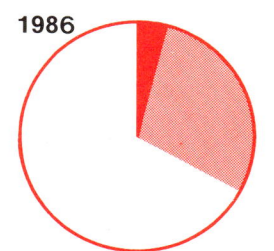
Total: 22 million

KEY
Primary
Secondary
Tertiary

I Grouping of industries in regions of Britain, 1986

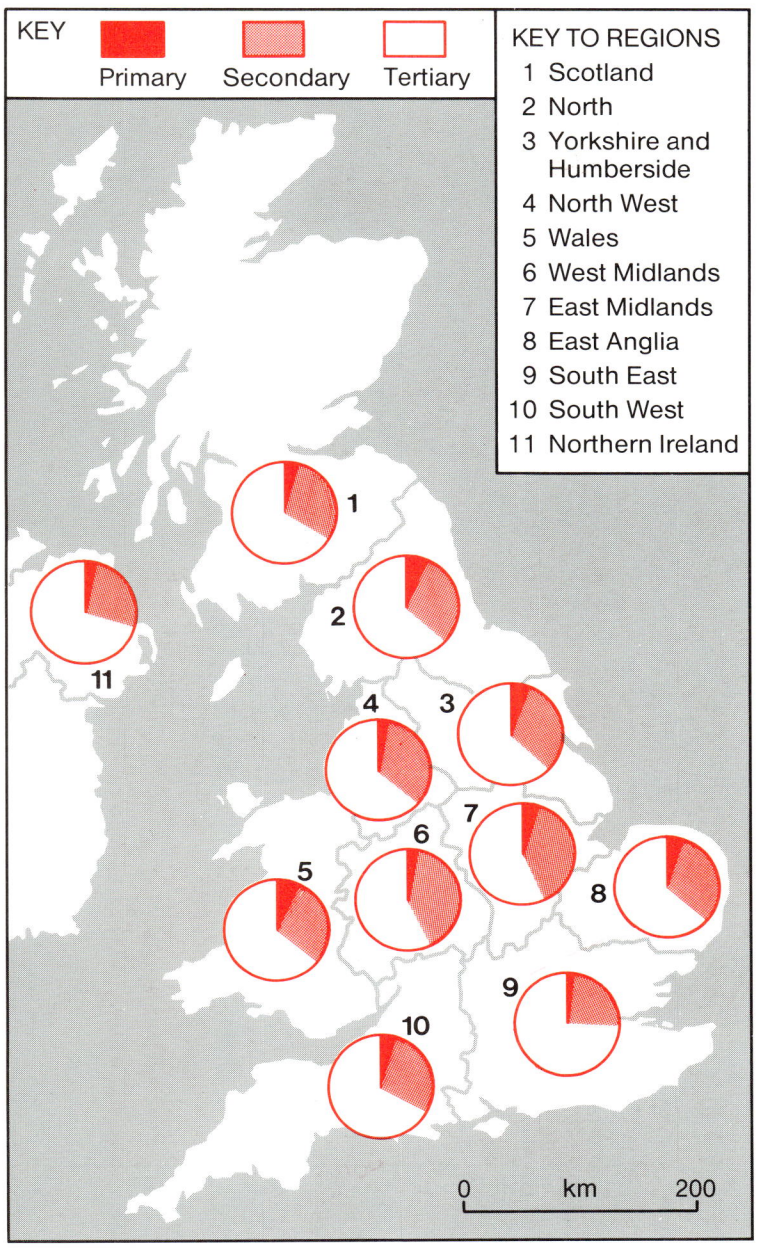

KEY
- Primary (red)
- Secondary (light red)
- Tertiary (white)

KEY TO REGIONS
1. Scotland
2. North
3. Yorkshire and Humberside
4. North West
5. Wales
6. West Midlands
7. East Midlands
8. East Anglia
9. South East
10. South West
11. Northern Ireland

0   km   200

Work unit

Look at the pie charts and information in diagram H.

1. (a) In which year was the total number of workers greatest?
   (b) How many workers were there that year?
2. (a) In which year was the proportion of workers in primary industry greatest?
   (b) In which year was the proportion of workers in secondary industry greatest?
   (c) In which year was the proportion of workers in tertiary industry greatest?
3. Look at map I and the 1981 pie chart in diagram H.
   (a) Name one region which has a very similar industry pie chart to the one for Britain as a whole.
   (b) Name one region which has quite a different industry pie chart from the one for Britain as whole.
4. Look at graph J. It has been drawn to show the change in the total number of workers in Britain between 1841 and 1981. Copy the graph and complete it using the information in diagram H.
5. Look at pie chart K. Each mark on the edge stands for 1%. Copy and complete the pie chart to show the information for 1960 in Table 1. Shade your chart and give it a key.
6. How have the percentages of workers in the three groups of industry changed between 1960 and 1980 (see Table 1)?
7. Why do you think that the proportion of workers in tertiary industries increases as a country becomes wealthier?

J Total number of workers in Britain, 1841–1981

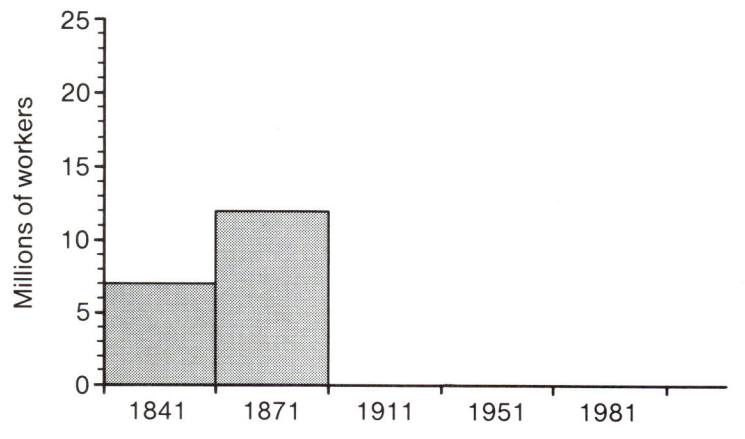

Millions of workers (0–25)
Years: 1841, 1871, 1911, 1951, 1981

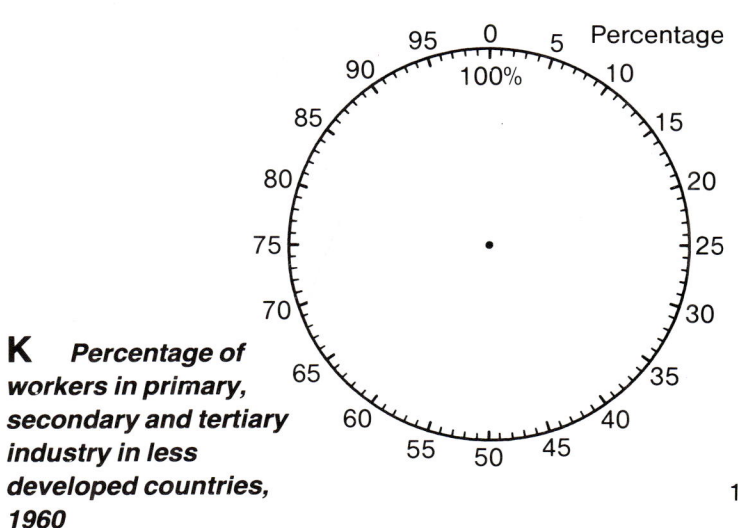

K Percentage of workers in primary, secondary and tertiary industry in less developed countries, 1960

Percentage

Needs in industrial society

Most people have heard of the book *Robinson Crusoe* by Daniel Defoe. It is based on the real life story of a Scotsman called Alexander Selkirk. He was marooned on an island in the Pacific. On the island, Selkirk's needs were simple, as cartoon A shows. He wanted only to survive.

People in Britain today need and expect much more. We own a wide range of goods which we feel are necessary to modern living. We expect **services** such as running water, electricity, gas, public transport to be provided for us.

The things we cannot live without are called *necessities* (for example, food, clothing). Things which make life more pleasant but are not essential are called *luxuries* (for example, cars, television). People who are able to buy luxuries have a fairly high *standard of living*. (Our standard of living means how well off we are.) Those who can only afford necessities have a low standard of living.

The number of goods and services that people are able to spend money on depends on how much they earn. People's standard of living therefore depends on their **income**. But if prices of goods and services change, this can also affect our standard of living, as diagram C shows. (Taxes paid to the government also affect our standard of living.)

Work unit

1 What were Alexander Selkirk's three basic needs (see cartoon A)?
2 (a) Which of the goods and services in graph B are necessities?
 (b) Which are luxuries?
3 (a) Look at graph B. Name six things for which family spending has changed by 3% or more between 1959 and 1981.
 (b) Choose two of the six things you listed in (a). Say why you think that change happened.
4 What is meant by 'standard of living'?
5 Is increase in income the only thing that affects our standard of living? Give a reason.
6 If your income increases by 10% and prices increase by 5%, are you better or worse off?

A

B *Percentage of family spending on goods and services*

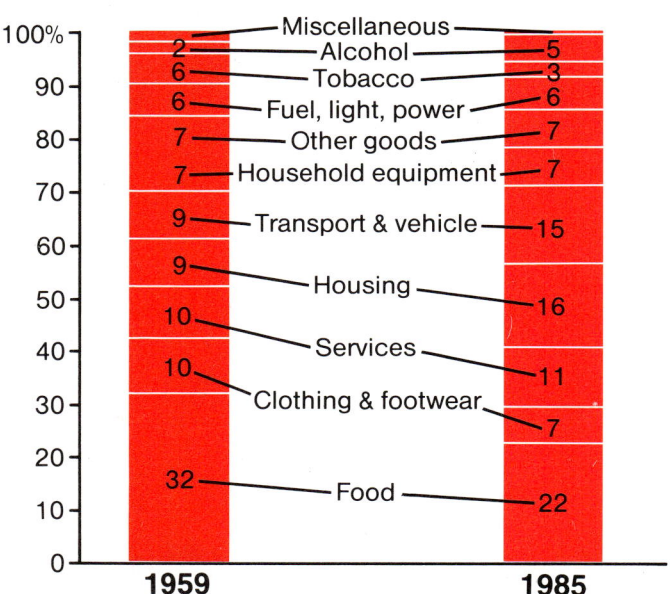

	1959	1985
Miscellaneous	2	5
Alcohol	6	3
Tobacco	6	6
Fuel, light, power	7	7
Other goods	7	7
Household equipment	9	15
Transport & vehicle	9	16
Housing	10	11
Services	10	7
Clothing & footwear	32	22
Food		

C *Relations between income and prices*

Income +5%   Prices +5%   **Standard of living**   **Steady**

Income +5%   Prices +1%   **Standard of living**   **Rises**

Income +5%   Prices +10%   **Standard of living**   **Falls**

12

Sean is 18 and unemployed. He lives in a one-room flat in Aberdeen. His only income is **Supplementary Benefit**. This is how he describes a day in his life.

9.00 a.m.	Got up, and had tea and toast for breakfast.
9.30 a.m.	Went by bus to the Job Centre to sign on.
10.40 a.m.	Stopped off in town to get some cheese and eggs, and to pay the rent. Bought a cup of coffee and a Mars bar — my daily luxury!
11.00 a.m.	Bought two new pairs of socks — my others have worn through.
12.30 p.m.	Lunch at home — a beefburger roll.
1.00 p.m.	Watched TV and stared at the ceiling.
2.00 p.m.	Tidied the flat. At least housework breaks the boredom!
3–5 p.m.	TV again! But I'd go mad without it.
5.30 p.m.	Fed the electricity meter. I have to be careful not to spend too much.
5.35 p.m.	Made a potato omelette to eat.
6.30 p.m.	Settled down to watch TV again but became depressed.
6.35 p.m.	Went to the pub and had one pint with my mates. It cheered me up. Couldn't afford to buy more though.
9.08 pm	Watched TV until the meter ran out. Went to bed. Dropped off to sleep about 11.30.

Jean is 38 and a part-time computer operator. Her husband is regional sales manager of a large **firm**. They have three children and live in Edinburgh. This is how Jean describes a day in her life.

7.30 a.m.	Got up and cooked breakfast for the family.
8.30 a.m.	Took the children to school in my car.
8.45 a.m.	Filled the car up with petrol. Then went to work.
12.30 p.m.	Finished work. Went to the hairdresser. Had a quick lunch in a restaurant nearby.
1.45 p.m.	Went to the supermarket for the week's shopping. Spent over £60! The 'box' of wine was a luxury.
3.00 p.m.	Appointment with bank manager about a loan for a new car. Agreed!
3.50 p.m.	Bought a new dress for the theatre tonight.
4.30 p.m.	Collected the children from school.
5.00 p.m.	Prepared the evening meal – 3 courses as usual!
5.30 p.m.	Phoned Helen to invite her and David back after the theatre for drinks and a light supper.
6.00 p.m.	Jim arrived home. Had our evening meal.
6.50 p.m.	Put the dishes in the dishwasher and went to get dressed for the theatre.
7.25 p.m.	Set the video to record 'Dallas' on TV. We'll watch it tomorrow.
7.30 p.m.	Babysitter arrived. Left for theatre.
10.45 p.m.	Returned with David & Helen for supper.
1.00 a.m.	Bed.

Work unit

1 Who has the higher standard of living: Jean or Sean?
2 Table 1 shows the goods and services used that day by Jean. Copy the table into your notebook. Make up a similar table for Sean.
3 Look at the goods and services in Table 1. In your notebook write the headings 'Necessities' and 'Luxuries'. Write each of the goods and services used by Jean under the correct heading. Then make a similar list for Sean.
5 Is television more important to Jean or Sean? Why?
6 How do the needs of (a) Sean and (b) Jean compare with those of Alexander Selkirk on his desert island?

Table 1   Jean's goods and services

Goods owned, bought or eaten	Services used or paid for
cooked breakfast	hairdresser
car	bank
petrol	theatre
weekly shopping	babysitter
box of wine	restaurant lunch
dress	
3-course meal	
dishwasher	
television	
video recorder	
drinks	
light supper	

Why here and not there?

Some **industries** are found only in certain parts of the country, and not in others. Sometimes there are obvious reasons for this. For example, coal mines have to be where there is coal under the ground. Shipyards have to be beside large rivers. Sometimes the reasons are not so clear, and they can change with time.

Iron industry: from Bonawe to Ravenscraig

To make iron, three main things are needed.
1 **Iron ore** (dug from the ground).
2 **Fuel** for furnaces. Early iron works used charcoal (made from wood). Now coke (coal) is used.
3 **Power** to blast air into furnaces. Early iron works used water power, and then steam power. Now electricity is used.

A *The furnace at Bonawe*

In the early 1700s there were small iron works on the west coast of Scotland. These were successful only for a short time. They could not compete with the much larger coal-fired furnaces (e.g. Carron). Over the years the iron industry moved to other parts of Scotland. This happened in stages as shown in maps B–E. For each stage, information is given about why the iron industry was *located* (set up) at that place.

B

STAGE ONE

Iron ore: brought by sea from England
Fuel: local wood for making charcoal
Power: water power
Finished iron sent to England by sea.

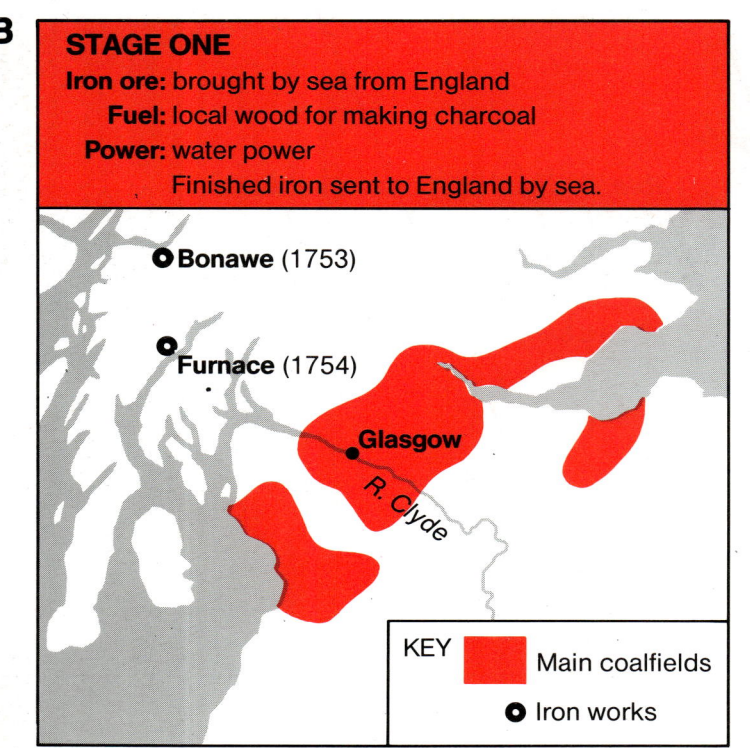

O Bonawe (1753)

O Furnace (1754)

Glasgow

R. Clyde

KEY
■ Main coalfields
○ Iron works

C

STAGE TWO

Iron ore: from local area and by sea from England
Fuel: coal from local area
Power: water power and later steam
Finished iron mainly sent to England by sea.

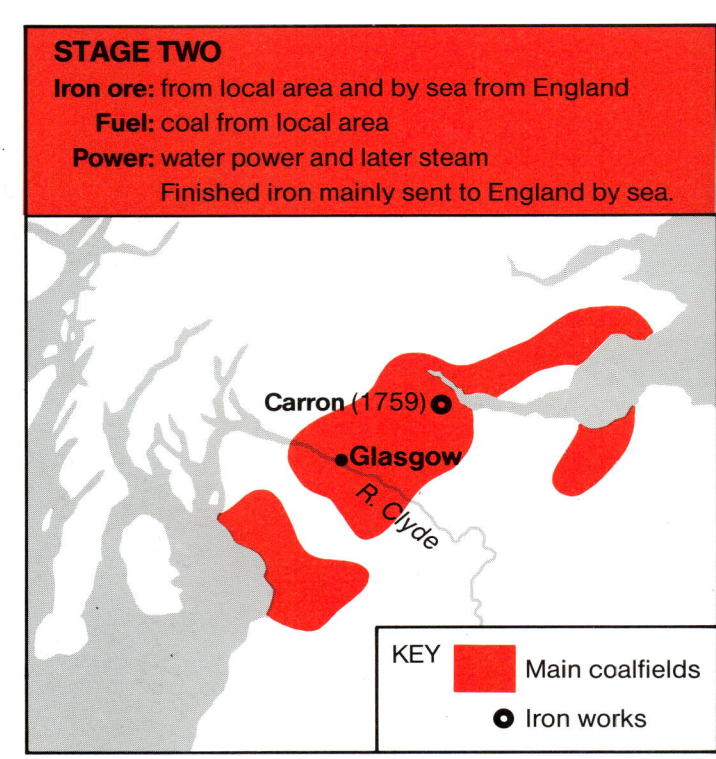

Carron (1759) ○

Glasgow

R. Clyde

KEY
■ Main coalfields
○ Iron works

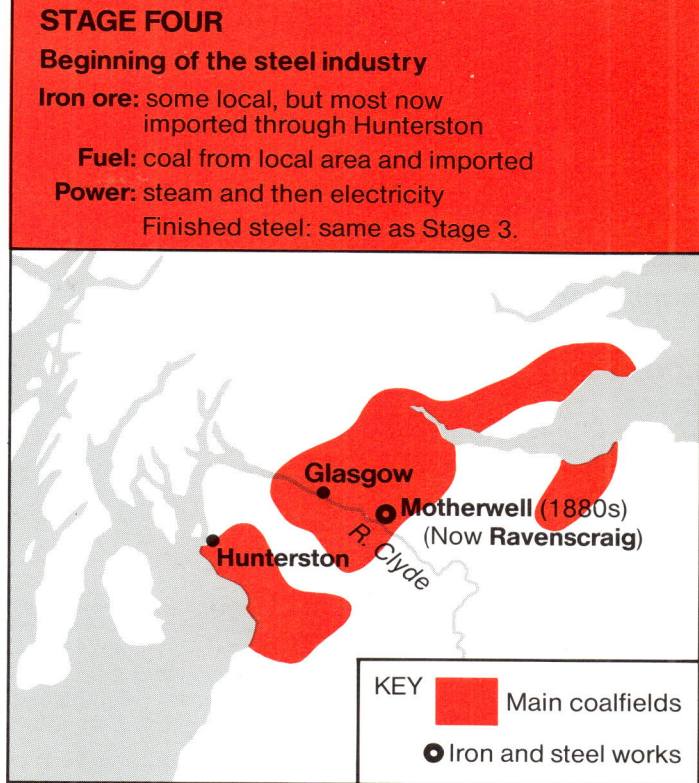

D

STAGE THREE

Iron ore: from local area

Fuel: coal from local area

Power: steam

Finished iron: high-quality iron used in Scotland in heavy engineering, ship-building and railways, especially in Glasgow and Clydeside. Much iron exported as well.

Glasgow • ○**Coatbridge** (1830s)

R. Clyde

KEY ▮ Main coalfields
○ Iron works

E

STAGE FOUR

Beginning of the steel industry

Iron ore: some local, but most now imported through Hunterston

Fuel: coal from local area and imported

Power: steam and then electricity

Finished steel: same as Stage 3.

Glasgow
○**Motherwell** (1880s)
(Now **Ravenscraig**)
Hunterston
R. Clyde

KEY ▮ Main coalfields
○ Iron and steel works

F *Ravenscraig steelworks*

Work unit

1 Copy and complete Table 1 using the information on maps B–E. Stage 1 has been done for you.

2 Look at picture A. How do you think air was forced into the Bonawe furnace?

3 What was the most important reason for the iron industry growing up in the central part of Scotland?

4 Why did the River Clyde become very important to the iron and steel industry?

Table 1

Stage	Place where the industry developed	Most important reason why	Other reasons why this place was suitable
1	Bonawe and Furnace on west coast	Plenty of wood to make charcoal	Beside the sea. Ships could bring in iron ore
2			
3			
4			

Branching out

If companies want to open up business somewhere, they have to think about the advantages and disadvantages of different places. This is true of **service industries** (shops, banks, etc.) and **manufacturing industries** (factories).

Chain stores, such as Boots, have branches in large towns and cities all over the country. They have to consider many **factors** such as the size of the town, other shops, people in the area.

Franklin's, an imaginary chain store, are thinking of opening a store in Denburgh. They have made a careful study of the town and the surrounding area. The information is used to fill in the forms shown in A and B. Seven factors have been looked at. Denburgh gets a point score for each factor. It can be one of three or more possible scores (given in the Points column) depending on which piece of information is correct.

Some of the information on the forms has been filled in. Some still has to be completed. To be chosen for a Franklin's store, Denburgh must get a total of 51 points or more.

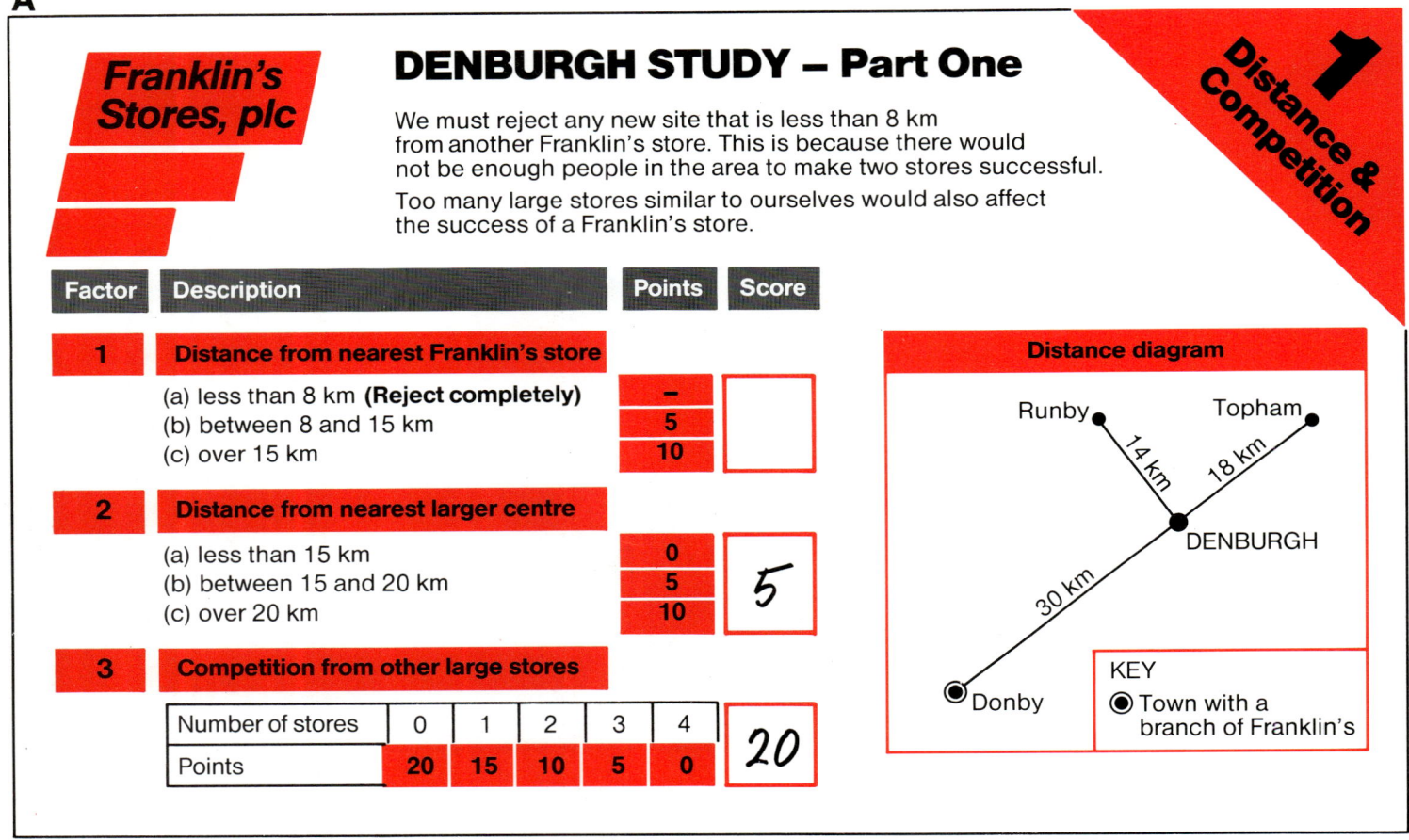

A

Franklin's Stores, plc

DENBURGH STUDY – Part One

1 Distance & Competition

We must reject any new site that is less than 8 km from another Franklin's store. This is because there would not be enough people in the area to make two stores successful.

Too many large stores similar to ourselves would also affect the success of a Franklin's store.

Factor	Description	Points	Score
1	**Distance from nearest Franklin's store**		
	(a) less than 8 km **(Reject completely)**	–	
	(b) between 8 and 15 km	5	
	(c) over 15 km	10	
2	**Distance from nearest larger centre**		
	(a) less than 15 km	0	
	(b) between 15 and 20 km	5	5
	(c) over 20 km	10	
3	**Competition from other large stores**		

Number of stores	0	1	2	3	4
Points	20	15	10	5	0

Score: **20**

Distance diagram

Runby — 14 km — DENBURGH — 18 km — Topham
Donby — 30 km — DENBURGH

KEY
⊙ Town with a branch of Franklin's

Work unit

1 Look at Factor 1 and the distance diagram. How far is Denburgh from a town that already has a Franklin's store? What score will it get for Factor 1?

2 Look at Factor 2, its score, and the distance diagram. Which one of Runby, Donby and Topham is the 'nearest larger centre' according to the results of the study?

3 Look at Factor 3 and its score.
(a) How many large stores are there in Denburgh?
(b) This could be good for Franklin's. Why?
(c) It could also be bad for Franklin's. Can you say why? (*Clue*: popularity of Denburgh as a shopping centre.)

B

Franklin's Stores, plc

DENBURGH STUDY – Part Two

To make it worth our while opening a new store, the population of the area must be of the right type, as follows:

(1) The population of the town must be above a certain size.

(2) The surrounding area should also have a large enough population.

(3) We prefer a younger population because they usually spend more money than old people.

(4) It is important that the unemployment rate in the area is low, for obvious reasons!

Factor	Description	Points	Score
4	**Population of Denburgh**		
	(a) less than 30 000 **(Reject completely)**	—	
	(b) between 30 000 and 70 000	0	
	(c) between 70 000 and 100 000	5	
	(d) between 100 000 and 200 000	10	
5	**Population of surrounding area**		
	(a) less than 100 000	0	
	(b) between 100 000 and 150 000	5	
	(c) between 150 000 and 200 000	10	
6	**Average age of population**		
	(a) younger than national average	7	7
	(b) similar to national average	5	
	(c) older than national average	0	
7	**Unemployment**		
	(a) higher than national average	−5	−5
	(b) same as national average	5	
	(c) lower than national average	10	

Population bar graph

Population (thousands) — axis marked 0, 30, 60, 90, 120, 150, 180, 210

Denburgh (≈60) ; Surrounding area (≈180)

Work unit

1 Describe the four factors which make a population the 'right type' for a Franklin's store.

2 Look at the population bar graph.
   (a) What is the population of Denburgh?
   (b) What score will it get for Factor 4?
   (c) What is the population of the surrounding area?
   (d) What score will it get for Factor 5?

3 What is the smallest population a town must have to be considered for a Franklin's store?

4 (a) Why do Franklin's prefer a younger population?

(b) How does the average age of Denburgh's population compare with the national average (over the whole country)?

5 What do you think are the 'obvious reasons' why Franklin's want unemployment in the area to be low?

6 What is unemployment like in Denburgh? (See Factor 7.)

7 (a) Work out the total score for Denburgh.
   (b) Will Franklin's open a store in Denburgh?

Your number's up

A Unemployment and vacancies: United Kingdom, 1972–84

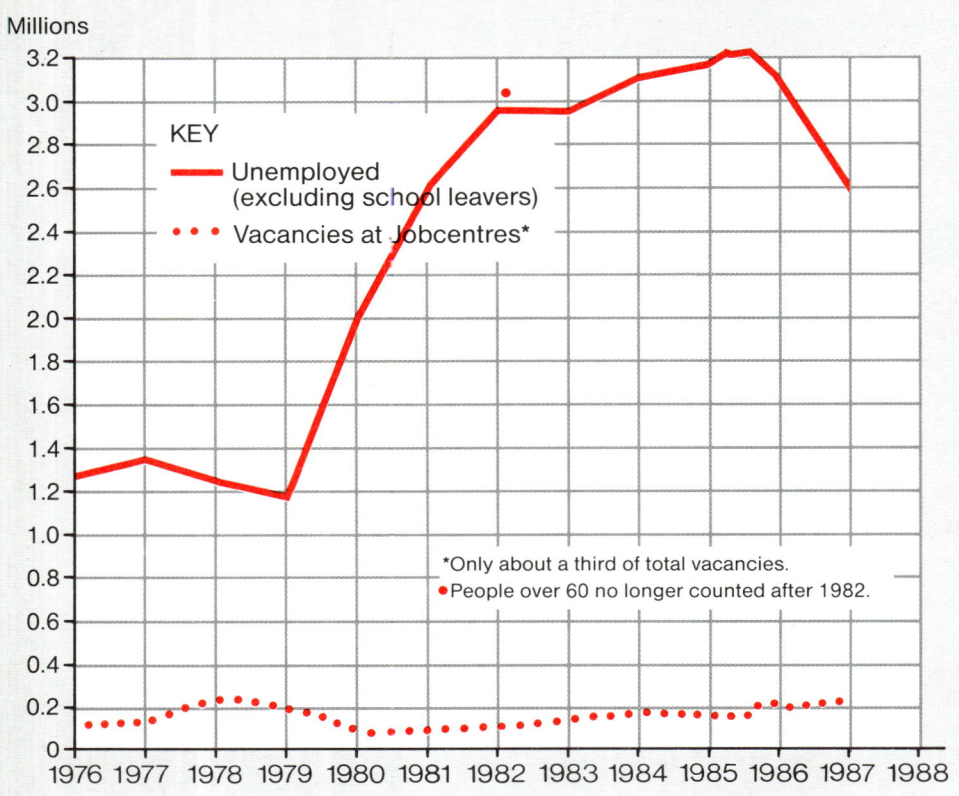

Millions

KEY
— Unemployed (excluding school leavers)
⋯ Vacancies at Jobcentres*

*Only about a third of total vacancies.
• People over 60 no longer counted after 1982.

(x-axis) 1976 1977 1978 1979 1980 1981 1982 1983 1984 1985 1986 1987 1988

B

Since 1979, unemployment in the United Kingdom has increased greatly. To be counted as unemployed in the U.K. a person must register as unemployed and claim **Unemployment Benefit**. Some people believe that the official **government** figures for unemployment are much lower than the 'real' figures. This is because there are many people who are out of work but who do not 'count' as unemployed.

For example, people who lose their jobs when they are over 60 do not count as unemployed. Others (such as many married women) are not counted because they do not claim Unemployment Benefit, although they would work if they could find jobs.

When the number of unemployed people increases it is not always a serious problem. If the number of **vacancies** (unfilled jobs) increases by the same amount, then there is a good chance that people who have lost their jobs will be able to find new ones. Unfortunately, as graph A shows, this has not happened in recent years.

Work unit

Look at graph A.
1. (a) Roughly how many people were registered as unemployed in (i) 1973, (ii) 1977, (iii) 1982?
   (b) Describe what happened to unemployment between 1973 and 1982.
2. (a) What happened to unemployment in 1983?
   (b) What information on the graph partly explains this?
3. (a) Roughly how many vacancies were there at Job Centres in (i) 1973, (ii) 1977, (iii) 1983?
   (b) Describe what happened to job vacancies between 1973 and 1983.
4. What information on the graph shows that there were more job vacancies than shown?
5. What information on the graph suggests that there were more unemployed people than shown?
6. Why was it more difficult to get a job in 1983 than in 1973? Give two reasons.

The **unemployment rate** is often shown as a percentage of the **working population** of a country, region or town. For example, in June 1984 the U.K. had an unemployment rate of 12.4%. This means that, on average, about 12 out of every 100 people of working age were unemployed. However, the percentage for a country or region often hides great differences within that area. For example, in June 1984 Strabane in Northern Ireland had an unemployment rate of 40.3%. Surrey had an unemployment rate of 5.3%.

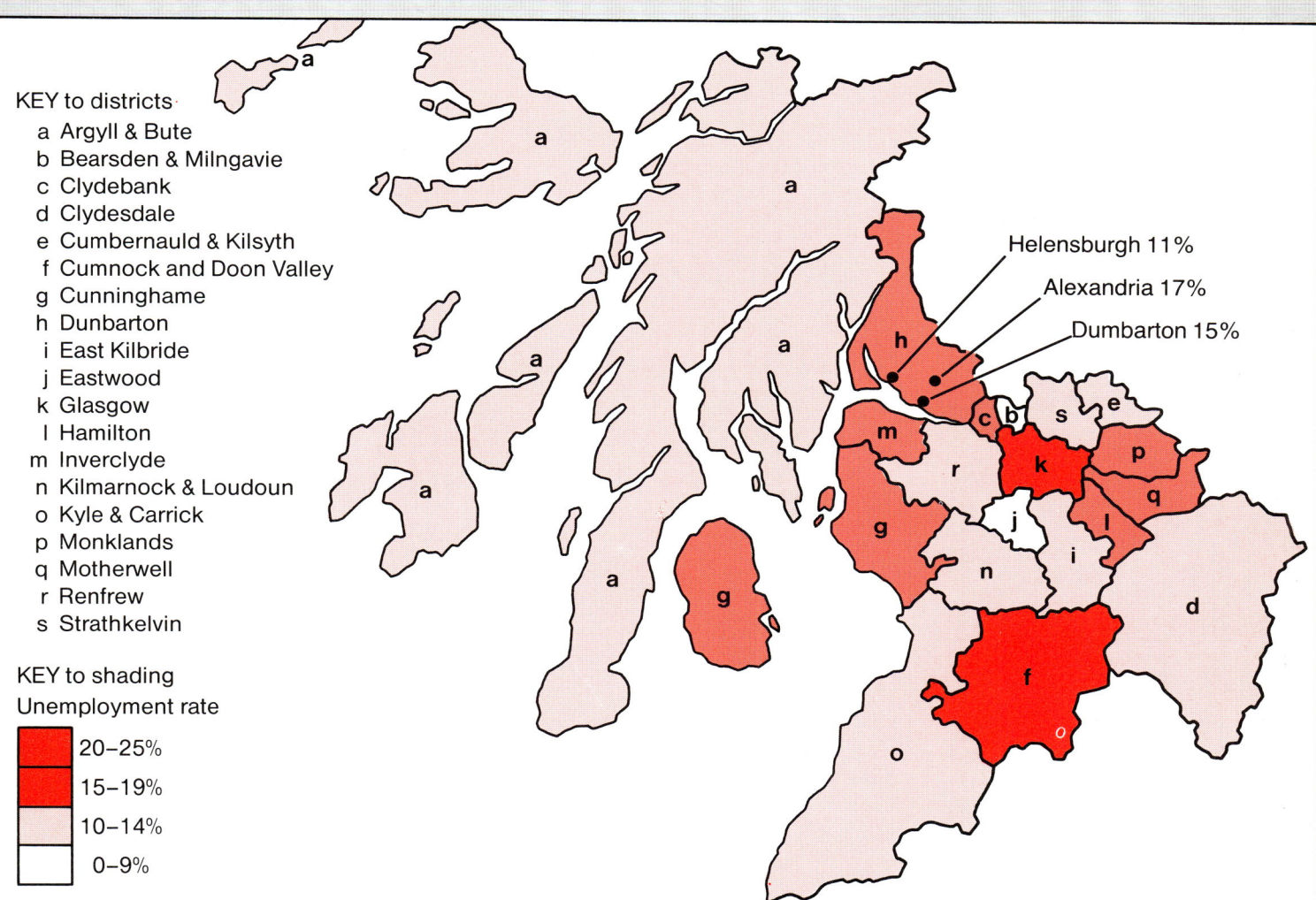

KEY to districts
a Argyll & Bute
b Bearsden & Milngavie
c Clydebank
d Clydesdale
e Cumbernauld & Kilsyth
f Cumnock and Doon Valley
g Cunninghame
h Dunbarton
i East Kilbride
j Eastwood
k Glasgow
l Hamilton
m Inverclyde
n Kilmarnock & Loudoun
o Kyle & Carrick
p Monklands
q Motherwell
r Renfrew
s Strathkelvin

KEY to shading
Unemployment rate
20–25%
15–19%
10–14%
0–9%

Helensburgh 11%
Alexandria 17%
Dumbarton 15%

C *Unemployment in Strathclyde Region*

Work unit

1 Look at map C, and the key to districts. In which district are the towns of Helensburgh, Alexandria and Dumbarton?
2 Look at map C and both keys.
(a) Which two districts in Strathclyde have the highest unemployment rate?
(b) Which two districts in Strathclyde have the lowest unemployment rate?

3 The unemployment rate for Scotland as a whole is 14.6%.
(a) Is the unemployment rate for Dunbarton *District* similar to that of Scotland as a whole?
(b) Is the unemployment rate for Alexandria similar to that of Scotland as a whole?

Work makes work

Britain has a fleet of submarines with nuclear weapons. It is based in the Firth of Clyde.

There are two bases at Coulport and Faslane, shown on map A. The bases are thought to add £60 million each year to the **economy** of Strathclyde Region. Many people are against nuclear weapons. They want the bases to be closed. But if they were closed how would this affect unemployment in the area?

A *Where workers at Coulport and Faslane live*

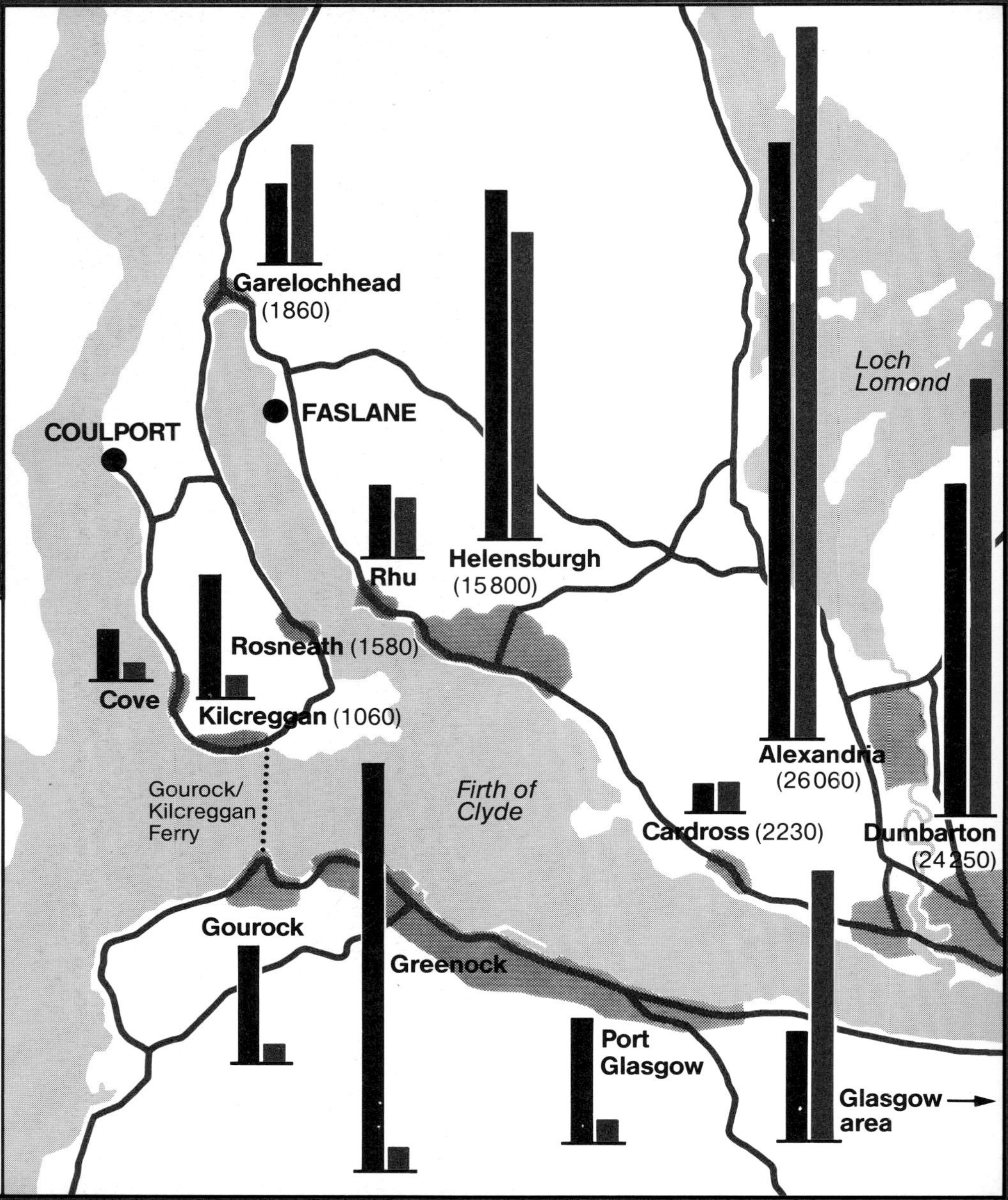

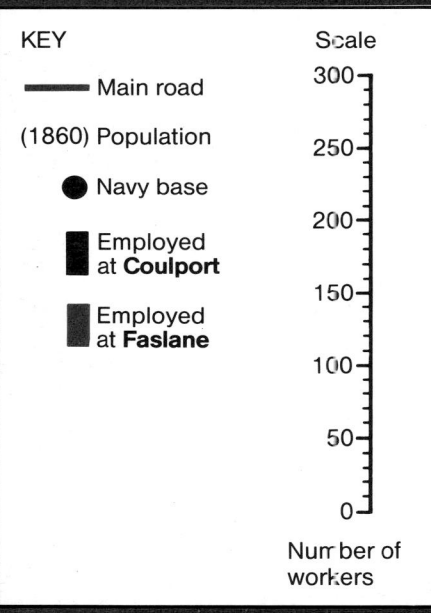

KEY

Scale

— Main road

(1860) Population

● Navy base

▮ Employed at **Coulport**

▮ Employed at **Faslane**

Number of workers

300
250
200
150
100
50
0

Garelochhead (1860)

COULPORT

● **FASLANE**

Loch Lomond

Rhu

Helensburgh (15800)

Rosneath (1580)

Cove

Kilcreggan (1060)

Gourock/ Kilcreggan Ferry

Firth of Clyde

Alexandria (26060)

Cardross (2230)

Dumbarton (24250)

Gourock

Greenock

Port Glasgow

Glasgow area →

Work unit

1 If Coulport and Faslane bases were closed, how much money would the Strathclyde Region economy lose each year?

2 (a) Using the scale on map A, work out how many workers from Dumbarton are employed at Faslane.
   (b) Work out how many workers from Alexandria are employed at Coulport.

3 Which town has the largest number of workers at both bases?

4 Which of the bases employs most of the workers from Gourock, Greenock and Port Glasgow? Why do you think this is? (There is a clue on map A.)

Apart from the Royal Navy workers, a large number of people living in the area shown in map A also work on the bases. They are in *direct employment* there. Other workers who deliver goods to the bases or who provide **services** there (for example, local painters or builders) are also said to be directly employed by the bases.

If the workers' families are taken into account, there are probably about 14 700 people in Dunbarton District who are **dependent** on the bases for their living. This large number of people live in different towns and villages in the area. Like everyone else, they need to buy things such as food and clothes in their day to day living. They need services such as banks and schools. Other people are needed to work in the shops, banks, schools, etc. (see diagram B). Therefore the bases at Coulport and Faslane have produced *indirect employment* for many more workers.

The number of workers in indirect employment is thought to be between one-fifth and a half of the number in direct employment.

B *Indirect employment from the bases*

Bus drivers

Teachers

Shop assistants

Doctors

Garage mechanics

Nurses

Taxi drivers

Bank workers

Hairdressers

Work unit

5 (a) What is indirect employment?
(b) Give two examples of indirect employment from the bases.
(c) What proportion of the direct workforce is the indirect workforce thought to be?

6 Suppose that the indirect **workforce** is half of the direct workforce. If the bases closed, how many workers would be affected? Choose from answers (a) – (c) below.
(a) The number employed at the bases.
(b) 1½ times the number employed at the bases.
(c) Twice the number employed at the bases.

Technology in Agriculture

Before farm machinery was invented, a large **workforce** was needed to harvest grain crops (picture A). There are four stages in harvesting grain.

1 **Reaping:** cutting the crop
2 **Binding:** collecting the cut crop and tying it into sheaves (bundles)
3 **Stooking:** standing two or three sheaves up against each other to let the grain dry out completely
4 **Threshing:** beating the crop to separate the grain from the stalk. This was originally done in winter.

Gradually machinery was introduced which allowed the same jobs to be done more quickly and with fewer workers. The reaper machine in picture B was invented by a Scotsman called Bell in the 1820s. It cut grain quickly and needed only one worker to use it. Binding still had to be done by hand for many years. But eventually machines were invented to do this job too. Even fewer workers were therefore needed.

Today most grain farmers use combine harvesters. These do all the stages of harvesting in one machine, including the threshing. One or two workers only are needed to use the machines. The machines work best in large fields.

C *A combine harvester*

A *Mowing corn with scythes*

B *Bell's reaper*

Work unit

1 Look at picture A. How many of the workers in the picture are
(a) reaping, (b) binding, (c) stooking?
2 (a) How do you think Bell's reaper machine (picture B) works?
(b) How is it driven?
3 After the reaper machine was invented, which of the jobs shown in picture A still had to be done by hand?
4 (a) What jobs does the combine harvester do?
(b) How do you think the machine does these jobs?
(c) How is the machine powered?
5 Why do you think combine harvesters work best in large fields?
6 In what ways is the combine harvester better at harvesting than
(a) the workers in picture A,
(b) the reaper machine in picture B?

Nine to Five

People who have full-time jobs spend a great deal of their time at work. They have to be at work between certain times of the day, five or six days a week. They only have a limited amount of time to themselves for relaxation or **leisure**, and they normally have little choice about when this will be. But the number of hours that most people work today is much less than it was in the past.

A

Bob Davies: a riveter on the Wear in 1918

'In those days, I got up at about 5.30. A big hooter woke us up. I had to jump out of bed and dash down to the shipyard for 6 o'clock. We worked till 8, then had half an hour for breakfast. Then we worked till 12 and had an hour for lunch. We finished work at 5. We did that Monday to Friday. On Saturday we worked 5½ hours.'

B

Agnes Limedale: an assistant in a Hull greengrocer shop in 1920

'We normally started work about 7 in the morning. We all worked on an outside stall. It had to be set up before 7.30. Lunch was a snack at the counter in the shop at about 12. It was one of the few times when we were allowed in the shop. At 5 o'clock we had a sandwich or a banana and then went on working. On an early night we might close at 9 or 9.30. Mostly we were open until midnight, six days a week.'

In offices and shops today, most people work regular hours, say 9 to 5, five days a week. Some jobs, such as farming, nursing or factory shift work, need people to work at times that others might find odd. People who do shift work are paid more than if they worked normal working hours. Some do not like the work, but others do. They prefer not to have to work the same hours every day.

C

Har Kiran: a factory shift worker, 1980s

I've been doing shift work for 24 years. I still don't like it, especially working nights. The shift system we use is:
Monday, Tuesday 2 p.m. till 10 p.m.
Wednesday 8 a.m. till 4.30 p.m.
Thursday, Friday, Saturday 6 a.m. till 2 p.m.
Sunday off

D

John and Liz Macdonald: farmers in the 1980s

We can't have fixed hours. In summer we're up about 5.30. Pea picking is from 6 in the morning until 10 at night. At haymaking time we won't usually finish until 9.30 or 10. In winter we get up about 7.15. If we go to the market with turnips we're not back till late. We can't get much time off really. The farm is our life.

Work unit

1 Look at extracts A and B.
   (a) How many hours did Bob work (i) each day (ii) in a week?
   (b) How many hours did Agnes work (i) each day, (ii) in a week?
2 What advantages and disadvantages are there in doing shift work? Make a list of each.
3 What advantages and disadvantages are there in the hours worked in farming? Make a list of each.

4 (a) Make up a list of questions that you could ask people to enable you to write a description of their working day similar to those given in the extracts.
   (b) Ask an elderly neighbour or relative to answer your questionnaire about the time when they first started work.
   (c) Using the answers given, write a paragraph describing a typical working day in the life of your relative or neighbour.

A farming township

A group of school pupils are on a field studies trip to the farm museum at Auchindrain. The route taken by the school minibus goes along the banks of Loch Lomond, over a mountain pass called the 'Rest and be Thankful', to Inveraray on Loch Fyne. A few kilometres further on, the road climbs over rough moorland. Then the pupils find themselves looking down on the remains of the farming **township** of Auchindrain. At the gate, they are met by the curator, Bob Smith.

A

Bob Smith Welcome to Auchindrain. What you see here is an example of a Scottish farm village as it was 200 years ago. At that time most people in Scotland lived in farm villages like this one. This is a typical house of the 1700s. The people lived at one end and the animals at the other. At first the houses were built of turf. Later, stone was used.

B

Pupil	Did they have to build the houses themselves?
Bob Smith	Yes. In those days people had to be *self-sufficient*. That means they had to do everything for themselves – build their houses, make their furniture, spin and weave to make cloth, as well as growing their own food. At that time there were no big towns, and very few **industries**. There were no cars or trains. Each village was isolated.
Pupil	What sort of food did they have?
Bob Smith	Not much variety. They grew oats, barley and potatoes. They would have a few cows to give them milk, butter and cheese. And some sheep for wool and a bit of mutton.
Pupil	Life must have been very hard for them. Was there no other work they could do?
Bob Smith	Yes, their life was not easy. But it can't have been all bad. Some families lived here for generations. Some of them would probably have earned a little money working at herring fishing, or at the iron smelting works at Furnace, just down the road. There would be some advantages in living and working in a place like this. The people here didn't have bosses breathing down their necks. They didn't have to 'clock on' in the morning. They could take a break from work if they needed one. People working in the new factories at that time had no breaks.

C   *The iron smelting works at Furnace*

D   *Inside a house at Auchindrain*

Work unit

1   The pupils who visited Auchindrain asked Bob Smith three questions. What were they?

2   Suggest three more questions you would ask if you were visiting Auchindrain, to find out more about life there.

3   Make up a table like the one on the right. List the good points and bad points which Bob Smith mentions about life in Auchindrain. Add two more points of your own to each column.

Good points	Bad points

4   Would you have liked to live in Auchindrain? Write a short paragraph giving your reasons.

New Lanark

In the late 1700s many new machines were invented. People began to work in factories for the first time. This was called the **Industrial Revolution**.

New Lanark is an **industrial village** in the central lowlands of Scotland. It was built for the cotton spinning industry during the Industrial Revolution. Map A shows the village as it was in 1863. Photograph B shows the village as it is today. If you compare the map and photograph, you will see that the village has changed very little in the last 200 years.

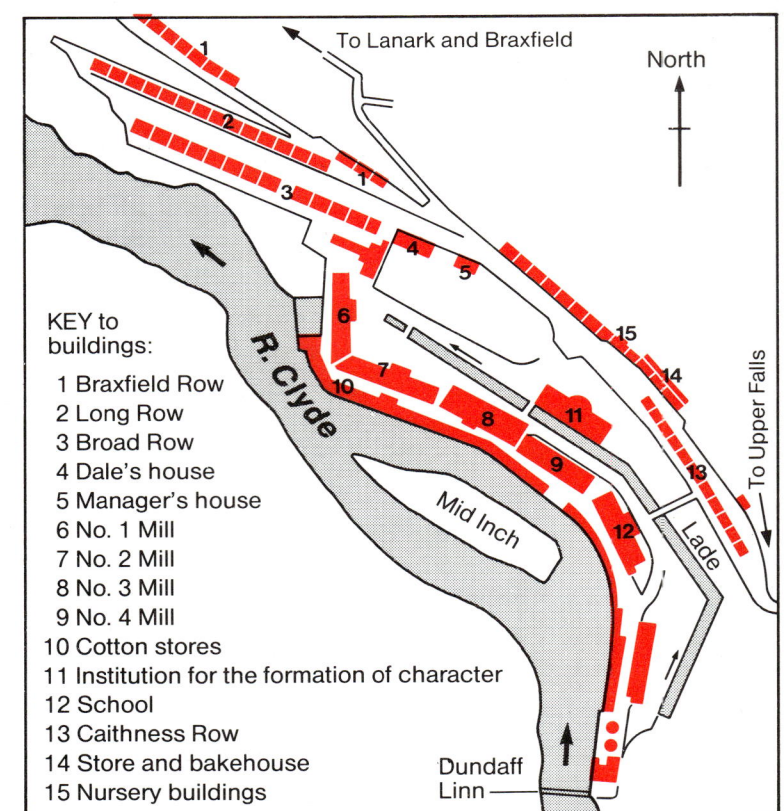

KEY to buildings:
1 Braxfield Row
2 Long Row
3 Broad Row
4 Dale's house
5 Manager's house
6 No. 1 Mill
7 No. 2 Mill
8 No. 3 Mill
9 No. 4 Mill
10 Cotton stores
11 Institution for the formation of character
12 School
13 Caithness Row
14 Store and bakehouse
15 Nursery buildings

A *New Lanark, 1863*

Work unit

1 Study map A and photograph B very carefully. Using the information on the map, name the following (labelled a–f on the photograph)
island a, river b,
building c, building d,
houses e, houses f.

2 There are four mills marked on the map. Only three are still standing today (see photograph B).
Which is no longer there?

3 In which compass direction was the camera pointing when the photograph was taken?

B *New Lanark today*

C *Water power, Dundaff Linn*

Why did Mr Dale, the original owner of the cotton spinning mills, choose to build them in New Lanark? The main reason was that the fast-flowing River Clyde provided *water power* to drive the spinning machines. In many other ways, New Lanark was not very suitable, as map E and sketch F show, but water power was a very important **factor**.

The force of the flowing water was used to *generate* (make) power. A *weir* (a small dam) was built across the river to make a powerful 'head' of water. The water then flowed through a tunnel into a special water channel called a *lade*. This provided a fast flow of water which was used to turn a water wheel. The turning wheel made power to drive the machines.

D *The lade, New Lanark*

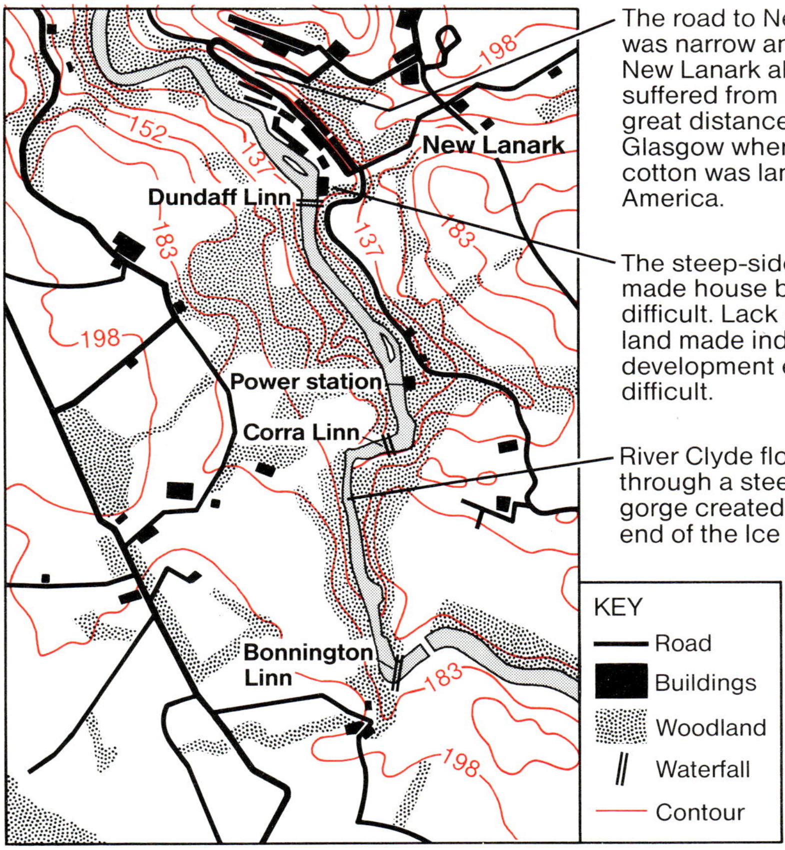

The road to New Lanark was narrow and winding. New Lanark also suffered from being a great distance from Glasgow where raw cotton was landed from America.

The steep-sided valley made house building difficult. Lack of flat land made industrial development even more difficult.

River Clyde flows through a steep-sided gorge created at the end of the Ice Age.

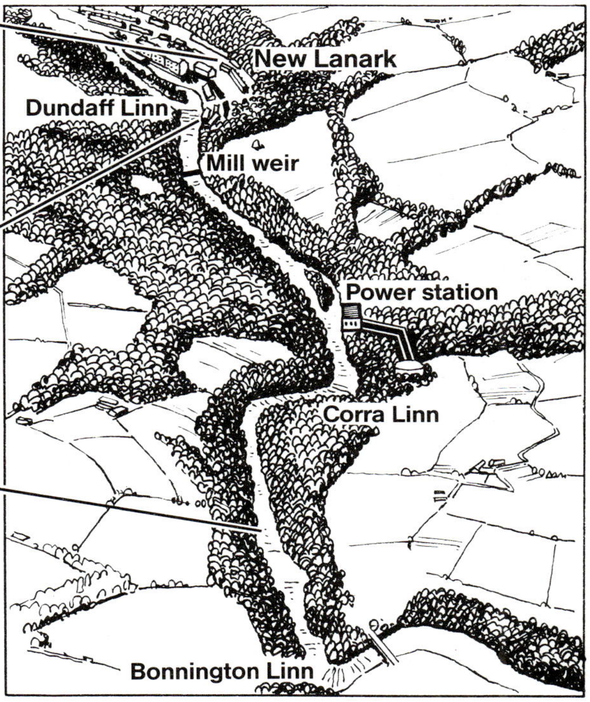

KEY

▬	Road
■	Buildings
▦	Woodland
‖	Waterfall
—	Contour

E *New Lanark area*

F *Sketch of New Lanark area*

Later, steam became more important as a source of power to drive machinery. Coal could be burnt to heat water and make steam. Industry therefore moved to coalfield areas. Places such as New Lanark became less important.

Water power is still important in the New Lanark area, however. It is now used to generate electricity. This is called *hydro-electric power*.

Work unit

1 Read the information in the text and illustrations. Make (a) a list of the advantages and (b) a list of the disadvantages that New Lanark had as a place for the cotton spinning industry.

2 Give an example of a natural feature marked on map E which suggests that the river could provide water power.

3 How can you tell from the map that the valley is steep-sided?

New Lanark's past

The Owners of the Mills

Arkwright: An English cotton spinner who invented a new machine for spinning cotton (the water frame). It needed water power to make it work.

David Dale: A Scottish cotton spinner and a friend of Arkwright.

In 1784 the two men visited the famous waterfalls on the River Clyde. Arkwright said it was one of the best places he had ever seen for building cotton mills. In 1785, Dale and Arkwright built the mills, and houses for the mill workers.

Robert Owen: Bought the mills from Dale in 1800.

The Mill Workers

According to a book written at the time:
- the place where New Lanark was to be built was a 'muddy swamp', and no-one lived there;
- Dale had problems getting workers to come to New Lanark. He had to persuade families from the Highlands to come.

Number of workers at New Lanark, 1811

	Male	Female
No. 1 Mill	150	408
No. 2 Mill	163	283
No. 3 Mill	112	286

Working Conditions

'The workers must turn up early on Monday morning when the water frames were started, work their 12 or 14 hour day and repeat this each day until Saturday evening – week after week, month after month, with Sundays off and perhaps 2 days holiday in the whole year.'

Adapted from T.C. Smout, *A History of the Scottish People* (Collins)

Because machines were used, women and children could do almost all the jobs in the factories. It was usual for very young children to be employed. Women were paid less than men. They were also used to doing as they were told in the 1700s.

NEW LANARK MILLS
NOTICE

1. Working hours cut to twelve
2. No children under ten to work
3. School provided for younger children
4. No worker to be whipped
5. Education for adult workers
6. Low prices at village shop
7. Good houses provided for workers.

Signed *R. Owen*

Work unit

1 Why did Arkwright and Dale need to build their mills beside a river?
2 Why could Dale not employ local workers?
3 How do we know that Dale was successful in persuading a large number of people to come to New Lanark?
4 (a) Were there more men or women working at New Lanark?
(b) Why? Give three reasons to explain your answer.
5 What evidence is there that working conditions at New Lanark were better than in other mills?
6 Look back at map A on page 26. What evidence is there in New Lanark to show that some of the workers came from the far north of Scotland? (You may need to use an atlas to help you with this question.)

Is small beautiful?

Firms come in all shapes and sizes. There are very large companies which **employ** thousands of workers. There are also many small companies which employ only a handful of workers. There are even some small businesses which are run from people's homes instead of in factories.

Before the invention of machinery in the eighteenth century, most weaving and spinning was done in people's homes. Wool or cotton was delivered to workers in their cottages. The finished work was collected later.

When machines were invented, this type of work died out. The machines were too big for people's homes, and needed power to drive them.

A   *Knitting 'outworkers' in the 1700s*

Knitwear from Balloch

Hermione Spencer runs a small business near Balloch in Dunbartonshire. Her workers produce high-quality fashion knitwear in their own homes. The knitwear is specially designed and hand knitted, so it is expensive. It is sold in shops in London, Paris and New York.

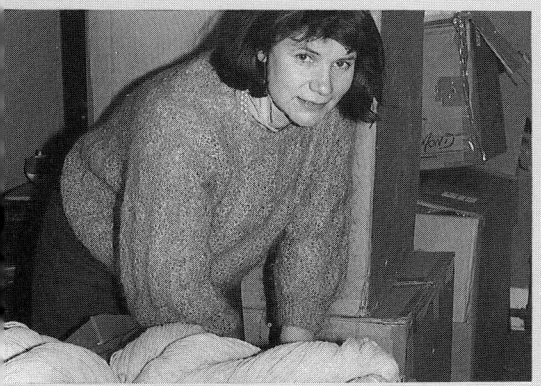

B   *Wool, the raw material for knitting, comes from all over the world. Mrs Spencer buys the wool and has it delivered to her home.*

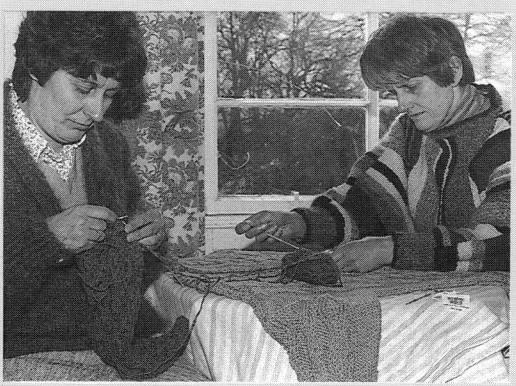

C   *'Outworkers' knitting for Mrs Spencer at home. This is highly skilled work.*

D   *Completed sweaters are sold to a wholesaler (£25–£50 each) who supplies them to shops such as Harrods (cost £70–£100)*

Work unit

1   When machines were first invented in the eighteenth century, why could they not be put into people's homes?

2   What are the main costs or expenses that Mrs Spencer has in her business?

3   What expense does Mrs Spencer *not* have because she uses 'outworkers' to do the knitting?

4   The difference between the *wholesale* price and the shop price is called the 'mark up'. Who receives that money?

5   It would be cheaper and quicker to make similar sweaters on machines. Why do you think customers are prepared to pay so much for Mrs Spencer's knitwear?

A woman's work

Women have always worked. Centuries ago, women and men worked together on farms. Women also worked at spinning in their homes. In the late 1700s, when machines were invented, large numbers of women were **employed** in factories. Many women worked as maids or cooks. Some women even worked in coal mines.

During the First and Second World Wars, thousands of men had to leave their jobs to go and fight abroad. This meant that suddenly the **working population** was much smaller than normal. Women were therefore employed in larger numbers than before. They took over many jobs which had **traditionally** been done by men: for example, engineering, making weapons, driving lorries and trams. During these emergency times, women also became **promoted** to better jobs. But when the wars were over and the men returned, women were expected to give up these jobs.

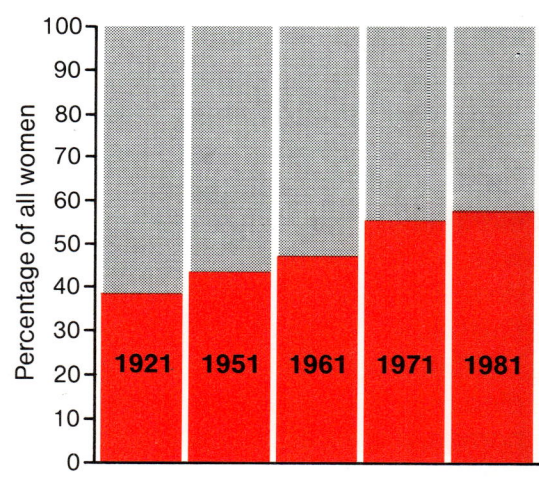

A *Working women, 1921 to 1981*

In recent years more and more women have gone out to work. However, the better-paid jobs still normally go to men, as Table 1 shows.

Many people still believe that men should not be typists or nurses, for example, and that women should not be bank managers or builders. But where do they get these ideas from?

Table 1 Working men and women in Britain, 1986–7

	Men	Women
Population	27.5 million	29 million
Working population	16 million	11 million
Average weekly earnings	£203	£134
Number of training apprentices	54 000	3 900
Number of other trainees	242 000	165 000

B *Are you being programmed?*

C

LESLEY – LONG DISTANCE LORRY DRIVER

'Have you got a single room for the night?'

'Yes, indeed, Madam.'

'Is it all right if I leave my vehicle in your car park?'

'Certainly, Madam.'

'It's the one with the 40-foot trailer behind it ...'

She telephoned or visited one local company after another. 'I'll be truthful with you, love,' said one old Doncaster trucker. 'There's no way I'm going to trust twenty thousand quids' worth of my vehicle in a woman's hands.'

It was always the same when she went into a cafe for the first time. The drivers all fell silent. Then they looked out into the park for a car. When they saw no car, they assumed she was a hitch-hiker and asked her where she wanted to go. She would then explain and wait for the usual handful of jokes about women drivers.

D

Making history as council apprentices

Glasgow District Council's direct labour department made history when they selected three girls from 700 applicants for trades apprenticeships.

Angela Shuttleton, 16, of Fernhill, Rutherglen, is a joinery apprentice who even as a small girl preferred toolkits to dolls. A former pupil of Cathkin High School, she got, with two other subjects, an 'O' grade in woodwork. She had no difficulty in being allowed to take the subject.

On the other hand, Fiona Duffy, 17, also a joinery apprentice, found her old school, Whitehill in Dennistoun, didn't encourage woodwork, although their policy changed – too late for her.

The youngest of seven children, including five boys, she was the family member who did all the odd jobs round the house. She said: "In my last two years at school, I thought seriously about taking an apprenticeship. Shops and offices seemed boring."

Have they come across problems so far? "At first everyone looks at you, but then you settle down and now we all get on fine," says Angela.

Fiona finds: "Other girls think it's funny to be doing an apprenticeship. Lifting heavy weights such as doors has proved tricky for Angela. But she says: "I'm getting used to it now, my muscles are building up."

Training co-ordinator Tom Hewitt explains: "They had to put themselves over really well and impress our trades foremen. They'll work in varied jobs and will also have to impress tenants as employees of the council."

Work unit

1 What kinds of work have women done in the past?

2 Why did the number of working women increase during the two world wars?

3 Look at graph A.
   (a) Is the percentage of women who work going up or down?
   (b) When did the biggest change take place?

4 Look at Table 1. What suggests that women and men are not treated equally at work? Mention two things.

5 Look at picture B. What kinds of pressures are put on girls and boys to make them think about certain kinds of jobs only?

6 What do you think is meant by 'women's jobs' and 'men's jobs'?

7 Read the stories on this page. What similar problems did Lesley, Angela and Fiona come up against?

8 Is there anything in Tom Hewitt's statement (article D) which suggests that the girls were not treated the same as boys at their interviews? Explain.

9 Carry out a survey of the staff at your school to complete the table below. Use the results for a class discussion.

	Male	Female
Number of staff		
Number of promoted staff (Principal Teachers, Head, Deputy Heads, etc)		

Them and us

In a workplace such as a factory both the people who control the factory (**management**) and the people who work in it (the **workforce**) want the **industry** to be successful. They should both have the same general aims. Yet what we hear or read in the news often makes it seem as though management and workers are in a full-time battle. Workers always seem to be on **strike**. Managers always seem to be threatening workers. In fact, Britain does not have the worst strike record in the world (see Table 1). Also, there are many companies where management and workers **co-operate** successfully.

A

Table 1 Working days lost through strikes (per thousand workers)

Country	1976–85
Spain	1120
Italy	1060
Greece	870
Canada	690
Irish Republic	690
UK	**500**
Australia	480
Finland	460
New Zealand	400
Denmark	210
USA	190
Portugal	180
France	140
Sweden	140
West Germany	50
Norway	50
Japan	30
Netherlands	30

B

Co-operation – the name of the game

By our industrial correspondent

Since the Japanese company Sanyo took over the Pye factory at Lowestoft to make television sets, they have increased productivity dramatically.

Noel Salmon, the personnel manager, said that their success was due to the good co-operation between the workers and management.

'We know we have similar aims and we work together to find solutions to any problems. We always try to avoid a "them and us" feeling between the management and workers. In some companies management get special treatment – more holidays, better canteens, etc. Everyone is treated the same here.

We all eat in the same canteen, work the same number of hours, and get the same benefits. Everyone wears a uniform, everyone clocks in and out, and we all have the same amount of holiday.

Also, we have a meeting every day to discuss production.'

The main fear that workers have is that they will lose their jobs. If working conditions are bad or pay is very low, one worker cannot do much about it. Workers often join together in a group called a **trade union**. As a group, they are more able to get better working conditions and a fair pay.

Recently, new laws have been passed which reduce the powers of trade unions. Some workers are afraid that we are returning to the way things were in the last century. At that time it was dangerous to join a trade union or go on strike. In the early 1800s unions were illegal. Even after they became legal, employers could take action against union members, as the information in D shows.

D

1837	Strike of cotton spinners in Glasgow. Four men sentenced to Botany Bay (Australia) for seven years.
1837	Coal miners' strike in Lanarkshire lasted for 17 weeks. The owners brought in thousands of hungry weavers to act as blacklegs* and gave them military protection.
1842	Four men in Dundee sentenced to four months hard labour for meeting to discuss wages.
1856	Scottish miners strike after they were told wages would be cut from five shillings to four shillings a day. About 40 000 men in the west of Scotland went on strike. They armed themselves with clubs to deal with blacklegs. Many were killed.

* a **blackleg**   a non-union member doing the work of union members who are on strike

C

'RETURN TO LAST CENTURY'
SAYS UNION BOSS

The 1984 miners' strike to stop pits being closed down enters its thirtieth week today. A miner's leader spoke against the police yesterday. He said they used unnecessary violence on the picket* lines. 'The riot control methods, especially baton charges, used by the police have led miners to fight back.'

A local police chief claimed that the police were not to blame for the violence. 'Miners who picket in large numbers outside pits are breaking the law. Only six are allowed in law. My officers have been stoned by miners.'

A union boss said 'Our strike is broken if the police allow "scabs"† to enter the pits. Pickets are only trying to put the union's point of view to members who are going to work. Unions don't seem to have any rights these days. It's a return to the last century.'

| * a **picket** | a person on strike who stands outside their workplace trying to persuade other members of the trade union not to go to work |
| † a **scab** | a union member who goes to work during a strike |

Work unit

1. Look at Cartoon A. Why do you think management and workers often come into conflict?
2. Britain is often said to have a very bad record for strikes. What does the information in Table 1 suggest about this?
3. What has led to more co-operation between the workforce and management in the Sanyo factory at Lowestoft? (See article B.)
4. Look at the information in D. Which of the punishments given to trade union members between 1837 and 1856 would not be given today?
5. Look at article C.
   (a) Why is the miners' leader unhappy with the police's behaviour?
   (b) What are the police chief's views?
   (c) Why does the miners' leader think that the happenings of the 1984 miners' strike were a 'return to the last century'?
6. Make a list of the similarities and a list of the differences between the miners' strike of 1856 and the 1984 miners' strike.
7. Look again at cartoon A. Suggest ways in which both the management's and the workers' aims could be met.

MAKING THE HEADLINES

Radio and television news programmes try not to present a particular political point of view. Newspapers, on the other hand, do put forward their own political views. Before a **General Election**, they often tell their readers to vote for a particular party.

A

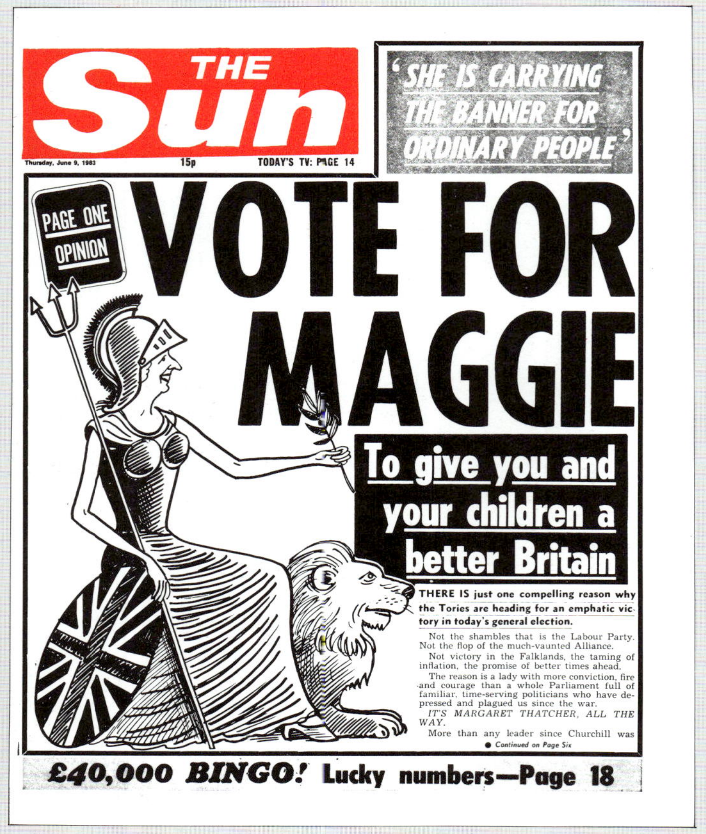

THE Sun

Thursday, June 9, 1983 15p TODAY'S TV: PAGE 14

'SHE IS CARRYING THE BANNER FOR ORDINARY PEOPLE'

PAGE ONE OPINION

VOTE FOR MAGGIE

To give you and your children a better Britain

THERE IS just one compelling reason why the Tories are heading for an emphatic victory in today's general election.

Not the shambles that is the Labour Party. Not the flop of the much-vaunted Alliance.

Not victory in the Falklands, the taming of inflation, the promise of better times ahead.

The reason is a lady with more conviction, fire and courage than a whole Parliament full of familiar, time-serving politicians who have depressed and plagued us since the war.

IT'S MARGARET THATCHER, ALL THE WAY.

More than any leader since Churchill was

● Continued on Page Six

£40,000 BINGO! Lucky numbers—Page 18

B

DAILY Mirror

(Eire 18p) Thursday, June 9, 1983 ★★★ No. 24,666 16p

STOP THE WASTE OF OUR NATION

..for your job, your children and your future

Vote Labour

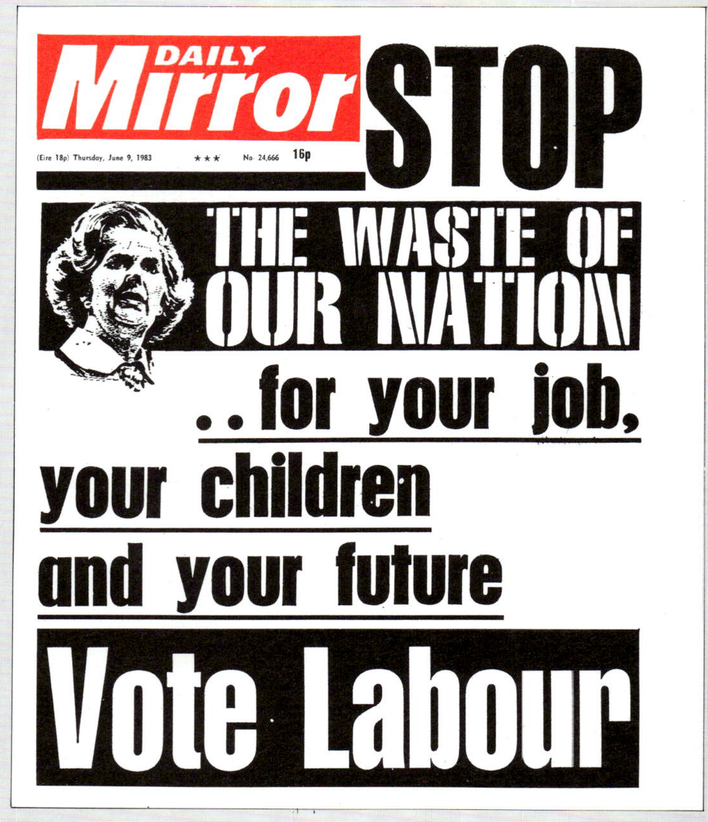

There is a close link between the Labour Party and **trades unions**. Newspapers which do not support the Labour Party do not usually agree with the views of trade unions. They make this clear in the way that they report news about them. Trade union members often claim that some newspapers report union stories in an unfair and misleading way. During the miners' strike of 1984 this claim was made about the *Sun* newspaper.

Picture C is a photograph of Arthur Scargill greeting miners at a protest march on 14 May 1984. A report about the march appeared in *The Times* newspaper of 15 May 1984. It showed this photograph with the headline '20 000 in miners' protest march'. The Sun newspaper had planned to use the same photograph of Mr Scargill, but with the headline 'MINE FUHRER'. This headline suggested a very different meaning to Mr Scargill's greeting (see picture D).

C *Miners' leader, Mr Arthur Scargill, greeting pit workers at a protest march on 14 May 1984*

D *Nazi dictator, Adolf Hitler, giving the Nazi salute. Hitler was called 'Mein Führer', meaning 'my leader'.*

Members of trade unions who worked on the printing of the *Sun* (called 'production chapels') refused to print the newspaper if the photograph was used with the headline 'MINE FUHRER'. They felt that the article would present a very misleading view of Mr Scargill. Picture E shows how the *Sun* front page was published that day.

E

Work unit

1 Which political party did (a) the *Sun* and (b) the *Mirror* ask people to support in the 1983 General Election?

2 Is the *Mirror* likely to support trade unions? Why?

3 Look at picture C.
   (a) Where was Mr Scargill on 14 May 1984?
   (b) Why was he there?

4 Why do you think Mr Scargill would have been very annoyed if the photograph and the headline 'MINE FUHRER' had been printed in the *Sun*?

5 Why did the *Sun* printing unions refuse to handle the photograph and headline?

6 How does the use of the photograph and the headline in *The Times* differ from the way it would have been used in the *Sun*?

SPORTSGEAR

Pat Mackie has just started a job with Sportsgear, a company which makes a wide range of sports equipment. The first three days at work were taken up with training. Before leaving work on the third day, Pat was given a copy of the company's *Worker's Handbook*. Pat has been told to read it carefully. She will have to do a short test about it in three weeks' time.

1 THE COMPANY

Sportsgear (Scotland) plc is part of a **multinational** company called Sportsgear International. Our headquarters are in New York City, U.S.A., but we have **'branch'** companies in four other countries.

Sportsgear International

| Scotland | Republic of Ireland | Hong Kong | Taiwan |

2 YOUR POSITION IN THE COMPANY

Managing Director (Victor Russo)
Manager Scotland
Personnel Manager
Supervisors

● YOU ARE HERE (But remember there can be no company without you)

GRADINGS: There are two grades of workers within the company
- **Hourly paid workers**
- **Staff**

3 HOURLY PAID WORKERS

Dress: Blue overalls
Hours: 7.30a.m. till 4.30p.m.
Payment: A rate per hour (e.g. £3 per hour) plus bonus which depends on **productivity** in the factory
Holidays: 4 weeks per year
Canteen: All hourly paid workers should use the WORKS CANTEEN ONLY.

4 STAFF

Dress: White overalls
Hours: Normally 9a.m. till 4.30p.m.
Payment: Salary (e.g. £8000 per year) paid monthly into a bank account
Holidays: 6 weeks per year
Canteen: All staff should use the STAFF CANTEEN ONLY.

5 THE MANAGER

Duties: Responsible for all final decisions regarding production, salaries and wages in the factory.
- Answerable only to the managing director
Note well: The manager is usually too busy to see workers.
- The manager meets with union shop stewards once a month to discuss problems.

6 PERSONNEL MANAGER

Duties: Under the direction of the factory manager. Responsible for:
- the running of the factory
- the hiring and firing of employees (a warning having first been given by a Supervisor)
- looking after the well-being of employees.

7 HEALTH & SAFETY OFFICER

Note well: The Health & Safety Officer is not employed to do this job full-time.

Duties: To handle complaints about health and safety in the factory and to take these complaints up with management.

Remember: ANY COMPLAINTS SHOULD FIRST BE REPORTED TO YOUR SUPERVISOR.

8 SHOP STEWARD

Note well: Your shop steward is not employed only to carry out union business but to work for the firm. The firm does, however, recognise the need to work closely with the unions. Some time is set aside for the shop steward to carry out union business.

Duties: To help workers who are still unhappy after having seen their supervisor about matters such as pay, timekeeping, behaviour, etc.

9 SUPERVISOR

Duties: To give out work to be completed.
- To make sure work, time-keeping and safety habits are properly carried out.
- To issue warnings to workers if these are not carried out satisfactorily.

Remember: THE SUPERVISOR IS THERE TO HELP YOU. IF YOU HAVE A PROBLEM OR COMPLAINT YOU MUST APPROACH HIM OR HER FIRST.

Work unit

1. What is a multinational company?
2. In what ways are the working conditions for staff better than the working conditions for hourly paid workers?
3. How is the method of payment of staff different from that for hourly paid workers?
4. If you were an hourly paid factory worker, who would you speak to about the following?
   (a) your machine breaking down
   (b) your machine not having a safety guard even though you have already reported it
   (c) getting an application form for a different job in the factory
   (d) complaints of unfair treatment from the management
   (e) campaigning for higher wages
5. Read the information about the Sanyo factory in Lowestoft (page 32). Write a short letter to the managing director of Sportsgear International (Mr Russo) comparing this company with Sanyo. Suggest any changes that could be made to improve relations between workers and management in Sportsgear (Scotland) plc.

The season's greetings!

Sportsgear have a monthly newsletter for the staff, called *Sports-talk*. A few times in the last year, it has mentioned money problems faced by the company. The company found it hard to sell their most expensive equipment when people had little money to spare. High unemployment had caused sales of sports equipment to fall. The workers were not too worried, however. The company had gone through hard times before. Sales had always picked up again and they would do this time too, they were sure.

The union **shop stewards** were called to a special meeting with the manager just before Christmas. They assumed it was about the drop in sales after the Christmas rush. It would probably involve decisions about changing to cheaper **production** methods in the factory.

The shop stewards were surprised to see a television and a video machine in the manager's office.

Manager: (*nervously*) I have orders from our New York headquarters to show you this video. (*He puts the video into the machine and switches on.*) Victor Russo, our managing director, has a special message for us.

Moira: (a shop steward): A Christmas message! Isn't this unusual!

Keith: (another shop steward): Really nice – if it's just Merry Christmas. But I wonder if there is more to it?

(*The video crackles into life; the face of Victor Russo, the managing director, appears on the screen.*)

Victor: Greetings, friends! It is so nice to be able to talk to my workers. You all know I look on you as my own huge family. First of all, I have a special gift for you all. A Christmas tree like this one is being delivered at this moment to . . . .

Keith: What a nice thing to do . . . .

Victor: Unfortunately, as you all know, the last few years have not been good for sports manufacturers . . . Now the Christmas stock is out, I'm afraid things look bad.

Moira: This isn't what I expected! What's coming now?

Victor: So it is with great sadness that the company feels we are forced to cut back . . . save money . . . cut corners . . .

Keith: We'll not get a bonus this year! But the jobs will be OK.

Moira: Yes, they couldn't throw people out at Christmas.

Victor: This unfortunately means **redundancy** for workers in the factories I have just mentioned ...

Manager: (*startled*) What was that? (*he reruns tape*)

(*There is complete silence from the gathered shop stewards.*)

Victor: Our sad decision means that we must say farewell to some of our loyal staff at our British factories. In particular, our Scottish friends must be brave, knowing that their suffering will help the rest of our firm to grow. There will be generous **redundancy pay** for those in the factories I have just mentioned.

All: What? Never! Don't believe it!

Moira: What about *consultation*! No-one talked this over with us, before decisions were made.

Keith: Or **co-operation**. We've accepted new machinery and talked about changes before. Why not now?

Moira: Yes, usually there's *compromise* to be found – a bit of give and take on both sides can stop strikes.

Manager: I'm sorry. I didn't know anything at all about this. Perhaps the rest of the tape will explain things.

Victor: And so, friends ...

All: We've heard enough! We'll fight this closure all the way!

Victor: I must wish you the Season's Greetings. A very Merry Christmas to you all!

Work unit

1 Which people are normally involved in making decisions about Sportsgear International?
2 Who takes the final decisions?
3 What co-operation did Keith think had happened in the factory in the past?
4 What is compromise?
5 Which of the following is an example of compromise?
   (a) refusing a wage offer and going on strike
   (b) walking out of a meeting
   (c) deciding to accept a management pay offer
   (d) accepting a lower pay offer than you wanted but with a new free bus service to work.
6 What could Victor Russo have done
   (a) to consult the workers?
   (b) to co-operate with the workers?
   (c) to compromise with the workers?
7 Write the first few lines of a newspaper article about the proposed closure of the Scottish factory. The headline is 'WE'LL FIGHT, SAY WORKERS'.

Me and the microchip

You don't have to know how computers work to be able to use them. Most people in Britain use *microchips* (tiny electronic computers) regularly: in pocket calculators, digital watches, video games, video recorders, automatic washing machines. Not very many years ago, computers were so large that they needed a whole room each. Now, with the use of microchips, a microcomputer sits easily on a small desk.

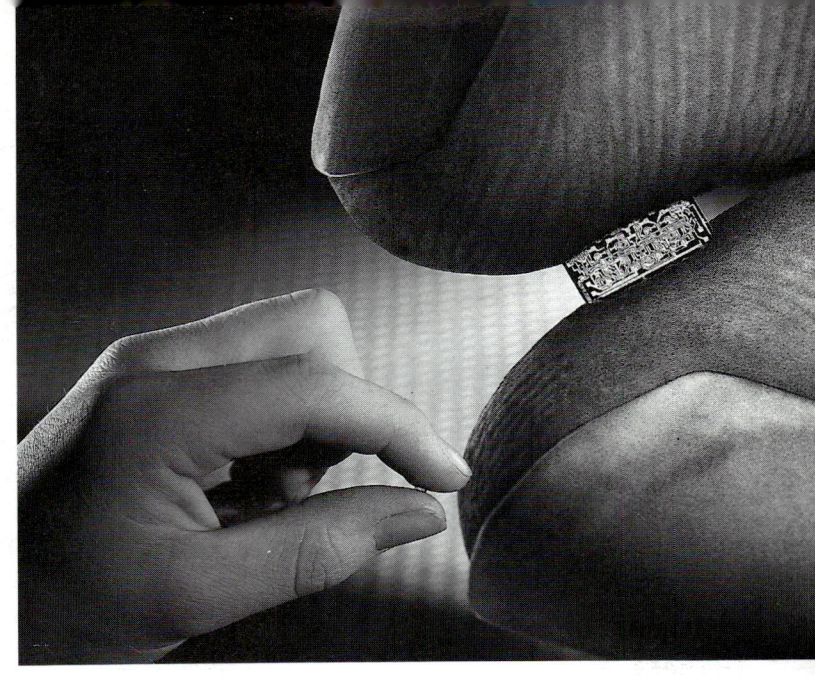

A *A microchip (enlarged)*

The microchip and the computer are going to change our lives completely in the next few years, as picture B shows. Some people are calling this the second **Industrial Revolution**. The **technology** already exists to make the things in picture B possible.

Satellites	By 1985 there were 37 Intelsat satellites in orbit. Each one can carry thousands of telephone calls and television channels.
Cable	In the USA and Japan, newly invented types of cable are being used to link homes with shops and television stations. People can even vote at elections without leaving their homes.
Microcomputers	Sales of these have rocketed in the 1980s, to ¼ million every year in Britain.

B *Home computer with a difference*

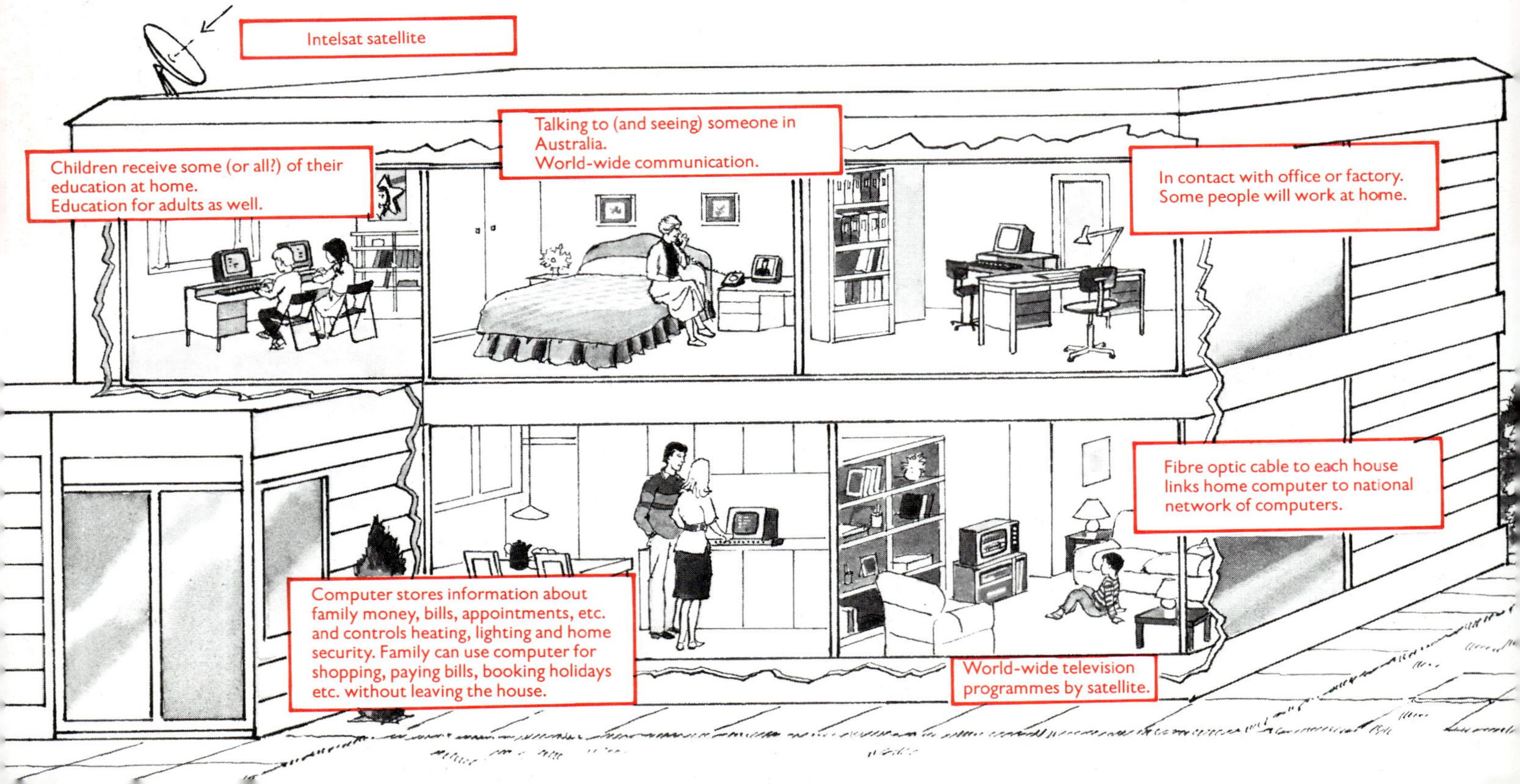

Intelsat satellite

Children receive some (or all?) of their education at home. Education for adults as well.

Talking to (and seeing) someone in Australia. World-wide communication.

In contact with office or factory. Some people will work at home.

Fibre optic cable to each house links home computer to national network of computers.

Computer stores information about family money, bills, appointments, etc. and controls heating, lighting and home security. Family can use computer for shopping, paying bills, booking holidays etc. without leaving the house.

World-wide television programmes by satellite.

Homelink

A large building society and a bank have joined together
to offer their customers a new **service** called Homelink.

HOW DOES HOMELINK WORK?

Thanks to advanced microchip technology and secret development work which has taken several years, it is now possible to link any ordinary black and white or colour T.V. set into the remarkable HOMELINK/Prestel range of services. Nottingham Building Society will provide a small console called a "Home Deck" that simply plugs into the aerial socket of your T.V. set. In many cases, British Telecom will put in the equipment and provide a demonstration.

For many thousands of customers, all this is provided free of charge. Without any further changes, it turns your T.V. set into a type of cable T.V. network that enables you to send and receive electronic signals and pictures. When you press buttons on the console, the signals go through your T.V. set, down your telephone line into a national network of computers and back to you the same way.

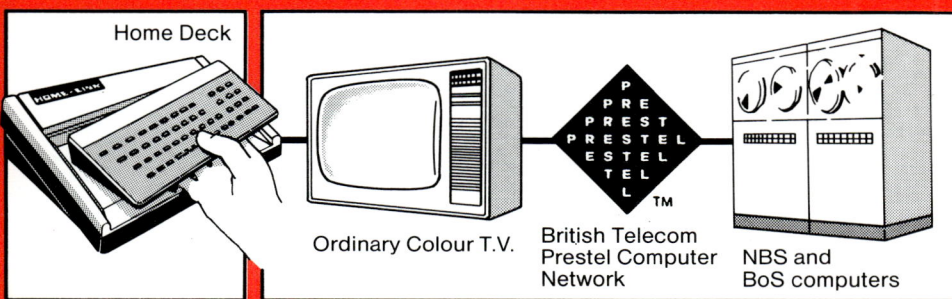

Home Deck

Ordinary Colour T.V.

British Telecom Prestel Computer Network

NBS and BoS computers

It's true: Homelink links your television set instantly to shops, banks, building societies, Prestel information, and other Homelink users.

You can 'bargainshop' from your armchair, choosing best buys, arranging delivery; actually bid in regular tele-auctions; book bargain holidays; order wines at special discounts; win Premium Bond type prizes – a prize up to £50 000 is planned; apply for a loan or mortgage. [loan to buy a house]

And you can do all this, and much more, 24 hours a day, 7 days a week – even when shops and financial services [e.g. banks] are normally shut.

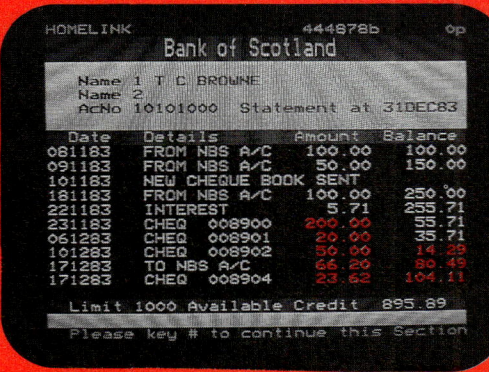

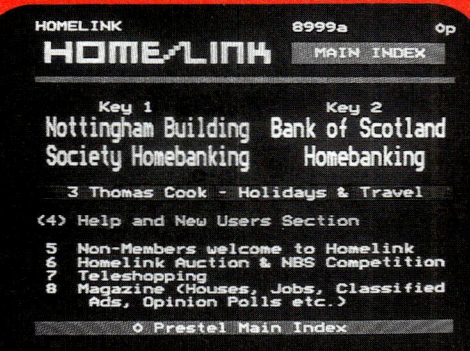

Work unit

1 Look at picture B. If homes do use computers in these ways in the future, will it mean people spending more or less time at home? Give reasons for your answer.

2 What two inventions (apart from computers) will make these changes possible?

3 Look at the Homelink information.
(a) Which building society and which bank are involved?
(b) Why do you think they chose the name Homelink?
(c) Can Homelink be used at night and on Sundays? Give a reason for your answer.
(d) The middle computer screen shows an index of services that Homelink provides. Name three of them.
(e) Look carefully at the bank account statement in the first computer screen. Does Mr Browne have any money in the bank? Or does he owe money to the bank?
(f) Write a short paragraph explaining why you would or would not like to have Homelink.

I robot... you unemployed

In the late 1700s new machines were invented to do work such as spinning and weaving. These machines took away the jobs of the people who had done the work by hand. Some of these unemployed workers blamed the machines for stealing their jobs. They broke into the new factories and smashed the machines. They were called machine breakers or 'Luddites', because it was thought they were led by someone called Ned Ludd.

The name 'Luddites' is still used today to describe people who are against the use of new **technology**, especially if it is going to mean fewer jobs.

A News has just been given in that you are an owner of those detestable Shearing Frames. I was asked by my Men to write to you and give you fair warning to pull them down. You will take Notice that if they are not taken down by the end of next week, I will send one of my Lieutenants with at least 300 men to destroy them. And also take Notice that if you give us the Trouble of coming so far we will increase your misery by burning your Buildings down to Ashes and if you have the Cheek to fire upon any of my Men, they have orders to murder you & burn all your Housing.

Nedd Ludd

B

THE LADS WOULD LIKE A WORD OR TWO WITH THE NEW COMPUTER.

C

Unemployment

In 1988 there were 3 million people unemployed. Some people believe that, as more and more computers and robots are used in industry, unemployment will rise to 5 million by the end of the century. One estimate puts it as high as 10 million.

There are many different views about the use of new technology in industries.
Not everyone believes that it will make unemployment much worse.

D 'British workers are not a bunch of Luddites ... according to some recent reports it is management that is the problem'

E 'With the exception of a few industries like the railways and printing, British workers have not tried to block the introduction of new technology'

F A recent survey of the effect of the microchip on Japanese industry says that:
(a) up to ½ million jobs will be lost, *but*
(b) ¾ million new jobs will be created by computers.

G 'The main opposition to the introduction of new technology has been ignorant management'

H A recent survey of 1200 firms in Britain showed that over half of the firms were not using or planning to use computers

Work unit

1 (a) What were Luddites?
  (b) Where did the name 'Luddites' come from?
2 (a) Look at picture B. The people in the picture are supposed to be present-day Luddites. Do you think they are workers or managers or factory owners?
  (b) Give a reason for your answer.

3 What is cartoon C 'saying'?
4 Look at statements D and G on this page. Who do they suggest is against the introduction of new technology?
5 Which of statements D–H does not agree with cartoon C? Explain why.

The technology used in **industry** is always changing and improving.
Most of the work done in factories can now be done by machines.

I Before 1700: goods made by hand with simple tools

J 1700–1900: power-driven machines in factories

K Mid 1900s: More complicated machines doing more work

L Late 1900s onwards: computers and robots doing most of the work.

Austin Rover Group Ltd

During the 1970s British Leyland, the company who made Austin, Morris, Triumph and Rover cars, nearly had to close down. By 1984 the company, now called Austin Rover Group Ltd, was once again a success story.

Problems

'The problems we faced were:
    low **productivity**
    strikes
    poor management
    out-of-date cars
    out-of-date machinery'

(*A. Barr, Managing Director Operations, Austin Rover, 1984*)

New technology

Investment in new models and machinery, 1979–87

Rover 200 series £40 million
Rover 800 series £120 million

Workforce
    1979 : 82 000
    1987 : 35 000

Productivity

'Our greatly improved productivity, the best in Europe, is due to:
    new technology, good management and a good workforce.'

(*A. Barr, 1984*)

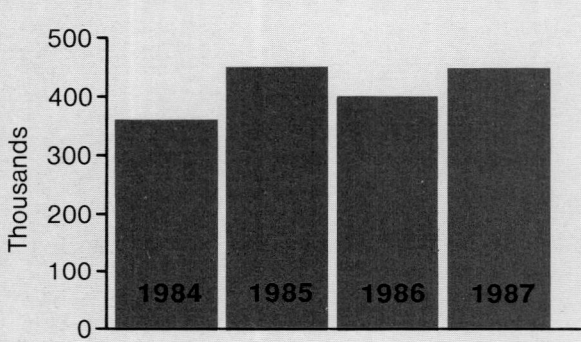

M *Total number of cars built by Austin Rover*

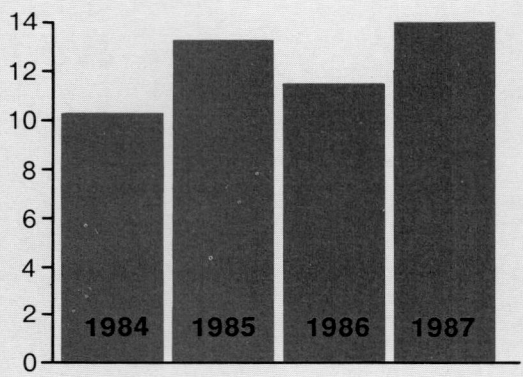

N *Productivity: number of cars built per worker each year*

Computers are used at many different stages in the production of cars, as pictures O – S show.
There is still a place for humans on the **production line**, but for how much longer?
Are we heading for the time when factories will be worked completely by machines?

O *Computers play a large part in the design of modern cars*

P *A computer controls the movement of all parts round the factory. It makes sure that each part reaches the correct place on the production line at the correct time*

Q *Computer-controlled robots weld the body panels together*

R *The Metro robotic body welding line*

S *Spray painting the car body: a dirty and dangerous job now done by robot*

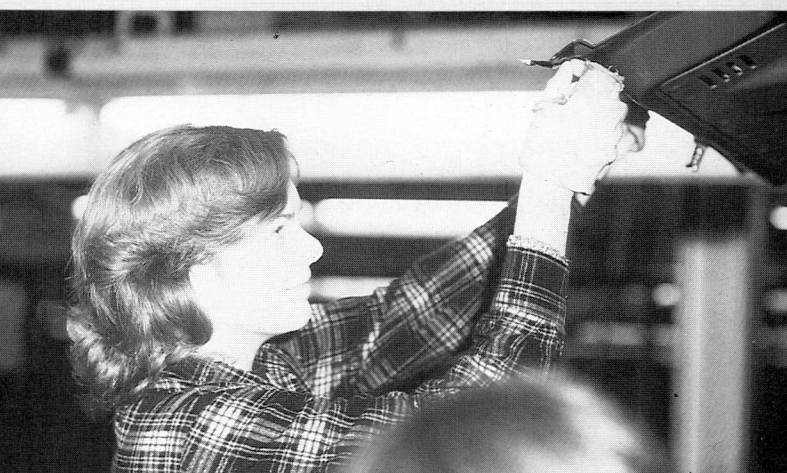

T *Hand work on the production line*

Work unit

1 Write down two examples of changes in technology used in industry. They can be ones which you have seen, or ones mentioned in this book.

2 Look at the boxed information on page 44. How many people lost their jobs at Austin Rover between 1979 and 1984?

3 What would probably have happened to the company if it had not brought in new technology and reduced the number of workers?

4 On a production line why is it important that each part reaches the correct place at the correct time?

5 (a) Write a newspaper story about the new success of Austin Rover. Set it out like a real newspaper article, with a suitable headline. Choose one picture from this page and one graph from page 44 to illustrate the story.
(b) Explain why you chose the picture and graph that you did.

6 Imagine that you have the chance to interview Mr Barr, the Managing Director of Austin Rover. You want to find out about the new machines and what the workers think about them. Write a list of the questions you would ask him.

Brave new world...
or same old problems?

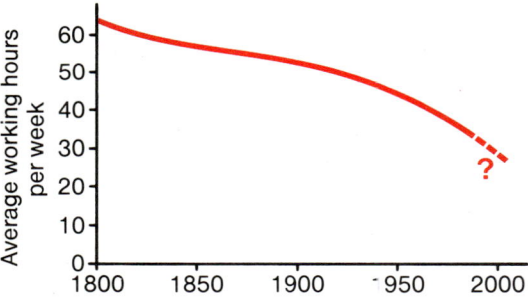

The optimistic view

Work will be more pleasant because machines will do all the dirty, boring or dangerous jobs.

People will not have to work as many hours a week as they used to. Longer holidays, earlier retirement and **job sharing** will also give people more **leisure** time. They will take up new interests, sports and adult education.

A *Working hours per week*

People will be paid not to work. They will be able to afford to enjoy their new leisure time. The money to pay for this will come from the **profits** of industries using new **technology**.

The pessimistic view

Unemployment will rise. The people with no jobs will resent those who are in work.

B *Unemployment*

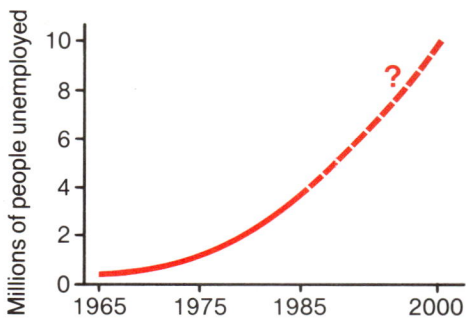

The unemployed will be bored and poor. They will turn to vandalism, violence or crime. There will be an increase in alcoholism and drug addiction.

C

Work unit

1 According to the pessimists, what is going to happen to unemployment in the near future?
2 What effect do they think this will have on the people who are unemployed?
3 Technology has been mentioned in another part of this book. Explain how you would find the page or pages where it is mentioned, without reading the whole book.
4 According to the optimists, even those people who have jobs will work less. Why is this?
5 The optimists believe that less work will be a *good* thing. The pessimists believe it will be a *bad* thing. Write a paragraph explaining why they come to such different conclusions.

Glossary

chain store	A company which owns stores in many towns.
consumers	People who buy goods or use services.
co-operate	Work together for a purpose.
dependent	Relying on something or someone.
economy	Wealth gained by a region or country from industry and trade.
employed (employment)	Paid to do a job.
employ	Pay someone to do work.
factor	A force, condition or reason which influences a certain decision.
firm	A business that pays people to make or do something.
General Election	When people vote to choose a government to run the country.
government	The people who run the country, led by the Prime Minister. It is made up of the party with most elected M.P.s.
income	The money that people earn.
Industrial Revolution	A period of history (1700s and 1800s) when new machines were invented which led to goods being made in factories.
industrial society	The people living in a country, or part of a country, where most people earn their living by working in some kind of industry.
industrial village	A small town or village which has grown up around a single industry.
industry	Work in which people are paid to make goods or provide a service, e.g. mining, car-making, banking.
investment	Putting money into something to make more money.
job sharing	Where one job is split between two people.
leisure	Free time during the day when people are not working.
management	People who take important decisions about the running of a shop or factory.
manual workers	People who work mainly with their hands making or doing things.
manufacture	The process of making something.
manufacturing industries	Industries which make goods (e.g. car industry).
mass production	Making goods in large numbers quickly and cheaply.
multinational	Operating in several countries.
producers	People who make goods or provide a service.
product	Something which is made, e.g. car, bread.
production	The making of goods.
production line	An arrangement of workers and machines in which each person does one job and the work is passed on down the line until the product is complete.
productivity	The speed of making goods.
profit	Money gained by selling a good or service after costs have been taken into account.
promoted	Given a job with more pay.
raw material	A natural substance from which things are made, e.g. wool, iron.
redundancy (redundant)	Loss of jobs because workers are no longer needed in a particular company or industry.
redundancy pay	A sum of money paid by a company to workers who have lost their jobs because the company no longer needs them.
service	Useful business or work done for others, e.g. serving in a shop, bus driving.
service industries	Types of work in which people provide a service for others, e.g. nursing, banking.
shop steward	A person chosen by trade union members to speak on their behalf.
skill	The ability to do something that usually requires training.
skilled workers	People trained to do a special job.
society	A group of people living under the same laws, e.g. British society.
strike	When workers refuse to work as part of a protest to management.
Supplementary Benefit	Money given by the government to people with low incomes.
technology	Scientific discoveries leading to improvements in industry.
township	Small group of people living in farms rented from one owner.
trades union	Group of workers who join together into an organisation to look after their interests at work.
traditionally	The same as it has been in the past.
Unemployment Benefit	Money given by the government to people who are unemployed.
unemployment rate	The number of people out of work divided by the total number of people able to work.
vacancies	Jobs waiting to be filled.
white-collar workers	People who do not work with their hands, e.g. office workers.
workforce	Total number of people who work in an industry or business.
working population	Number of people in a country (or region) who are able to work.

Index

References to illustrations are given after text references and are given by page number and illustration letter.